"*My Bright Abyss* is built of prose so lyrical and true you want to roll it around in your mouth and then speak it to strangers on the street . . . Wiman refuses easeful conclusions, he celebrates the verse and the two-faced joy at the hub of our lives—Nietzsche's *tragic* joy—and in doing so he has written what will be for many a life-changing book."
—William Giraldi, *Virginia Quarterly Review*

"Like the classic mystics, [Wiman] often resorts to a language of paradox to convey things that ordinary language can't . . . Wiman speaks carefully but powerfully . . . The best that can come from contemplation of mortality, perhaps, is a kind of wisdom that can give others strength—not by answering questions, like those best-sellers which claim to tell you what happens after you see the white light, but by asking questions honestly . . . *My Bright Abyss* is a book that will give light and strength, even to those who find themselves unable to follow its difficult path."
—Adam Kirsch, *The New Yorker*

"Burnished and beautiful, *My Bright Abyss* is a sobering look at faith and poetry by a man who believes fiercely in both, but fears he might be looking at them for the last time. Wiman's memoir is innovative in its willingness to interrogate not only religious belief, but one of its most common surrogates, literature . . . Here is a poet wrestling with words the way that Jacob wrestled the angel . . . Wiman calls his memoir the "Meditation of a Modern Believer," and it is that, but more than meditation, it is an apologia and a prayer, an invitation and a fellow traveler for any who suffer and all who believe."
—Casey N. Cep, *The New Republic*

"Without setting solace as his goal, [Wiman] nonetheless receives it; without offering the reader comfort, his book everywhere grants it. Mr. Wiman does not fall for the sops he sometimes finds in contemporary Christianity, which too often promotes 'a grinning, self-aggrandizing, ironclad kind of happiness that has no truth in it.' Faith for him has to do less with belief than with the acceptance 'of all the gifts that God, even in the midst of death, grants us . . . acceptance of grace.' The idea is a familiar one, but Mr. Wiman's [book] takes a new road to it. Perhaps every generation needs a writer to clear off this age-old path, renewing access and inviting entry, as Christian Wiman does in his weighty account of modern faith."
—David Yezzi, *The Wall Street Journal*

"The maturity of Wiman's voice, the quiet that suffuses his words and indicates his gravity of introspection, and the gorgeous cadence offered in damn near every sentence make this one book I'll relentlessly recommend to those peering into the terrifying and beautiful abyss—which is to say, anyone and everyone."
—Caitlin Mackenzie, *HTMLGIANT*

"[*My Bright Abyss*] blurs the boundaries between poetry and prose. If the nineteenth-century English poet and priest Gerard Manley Hopkins were transported to early-twenty-first-century America, this is the kind of memoir he might have written . . . This marvelous book, with its mastery and insight, its comfort and challenge, may well become part of our literary-theological canon."
—David Skeel, *Books and Culture*

CHRISTIAN WIMAN

My Bright Abyss

Christian Wiman is the author of six previous books, most recently *Every Riven Thing* (FSG, 2010), winner of the Ambassador Book Award in poetry, and *Stolen Air: Selected Poems of Osip Mandelstam*. He is a senior lecturer in religion and literature at the Yale Institute of Sacred Music.

Also by Christian Wiman

Stolen Air: Selected Poems of Osip Mandelstam (trans.)

Every Riven Thing

Ambition and Survival: Becoming a Poet

Hard Night

The Long Home

MY BRIGHT ABYSS

Meditation

of a

Modern Believer

CHRISTIAN WIMAN

FARRAR, STRAUS AND GIROUX

New York

For D. Forever.

Farrar, Straus and Giroux
18 West 18th Street, New York 10011

Copyright © 2013 by Christian Wiman
All rights reserved
Printed in the United States of America
Published in 2013 by Farrar, Straus and Giroux
First paperback edition, 2014

Owing to limitations of space, all acknowledgments for permission to reprint previously published material can be found on pages 180–182.

The Library of Congress has cataloged the hardcover edition as follows:
Wiman, Christian, 1966–
    My bright abyss : meditation of a modern believer / Christian Wiman.
        p.   cm.
    ISBN 978-0-374-21678-8 (alk. paper)
        1. Religion and poetry.   2. Christianity and literature.   I. Title.
PS3573.I47843 M9 2013
814'.54—dc23

                                                    2012021271

Paperback ISBN: 978-0-374-53437-0

Designed by Abby Kagan

www.fsgbooks.com
www.twitter.com/fsgbooks • www.facebook.com/fsgbooks

1 3 5 7 9 10 8 6 4 2

CONTENTS

PREFACE

Seven years ago I wrote a short essay called "Love Bade Me Welcome." It was published (with a different title) in a relatively small magazine, and it generated what was, in my experience, a lot of responses. It was later, though, on the internet, in anthologies, in church services and reading groups, that the essay acquired its second life, and I still get the occasional letter from someone who has come across it. These letters are diverse, intense, intelligent, and often from people who have no contact with the literary world whatsoever. They are the most gratifying reactions to my work that I have ever received.

And the essay itself? It was about despair: losing the ability to write, falling in love, receiving a diagnosis of an incurable cancer, having my heart ripped apart by what, slowly and in spite of all my modern secular instincts, I learned to call God. It was my entire existence crammed into eight pages. The essay detailed a radical change in my life, and then it seemed—or the reaction seemed—to demand a further one.

I am a poet. To be a poet in contemporary America is to be accustomed to, let us say, muted reactions to one's work. It is also—and this, I suspect, is not limited to America—to learn to write without much concern for audience, not because you don't want your poems to be read, but because in order for poems to honor the voice that creates them, a voice that, as even the most secular poets acknowledge, seems to come from "somewhere else"—in order, that is, for the poems to *be* poems—you have to acquire a monkish devotion to their source, and to the silence within you that enables that source to speak.

I'll never give up poetry—I wouldn't even know how—but all those letters in response to "Love Bade Me Welcome" made me more aware of an audience and my own need for dialogue. There is an enormous contingent of thoughtful people in this country who, though they are frustrated with the language and forms of contemporary American religion, nevertheless feel that burn of being that drives us out of ourselves, that insistent, persistent gravity of the ghost called God. I wanted to try to speak to these people more directly. I wanted to write a book that might help someone who is at once as confused and certain about the source of life and consciousness as I am.

Initially I thought this book wouldn't even mention my illness. I told myself that I wanted to avoid any appearance of special pleading, wanted to strip away the personal and get to ulterior truths. In fact, I think what I most wanted was escape and relief. During the years that I have worked on this book—which is very much a mosaic, not a continuous argument or narrative—my cancer has waxed and waned, my prospects dimmed and brightened, but every act and thought have occurred in that shadow. The form of the book reflects this, not simply the fragmentary and episodic quality, but also the accelerating urgency of the last chapters. I feel quite certain that I would be writing about matters of faith had I never gotten sick—the obsession is everywhere in my earlier work—but I also suspect that without the impetus of serious illness, my work would not have taken the particular form that it has. It seemed dishonest to avoid this dynamic.

When my life broke open seven years ago, I knew very well that I believed in something. Exactly *what* I believed, however, was considerably less clear. So I set out to answer that question, though I have come to realize that the real question—the real difficulty—is how, not what. How do you answer that burn of being? What might it mean for your life—and for your death—to acknowledge that insistent, persistent ghost?

MY BRIGHT ABYSS

MY BRIGHT ABYSS

My God my bright abyss
into which all my longing will not go
once more I come to the edge of all I know
and believing nothing believe in this:

✤ ✤ ✤

And there the poem ends. Or fails, rather, for in the several years
since I first wrote that stanza I have been trying to feel my way—to
will my way—into its ending. Poems in general are not especially
susceptible to the will, but this one, for obvious reasons, has proved
particularly intractable. As if it weren't hard enough to articulate
one's belief, I seem to have wanted to distill it into a single stanza.
Still, that is the way I have usually known my own mind, feeling
through the sounds of words to the forms they make, and through
the forms they make to the forms of life that are beyond them. And I
have always believed in that "beyond," even during the long years when
I would not acknowledge God. I have expected something similar
here. I have wanted some image to open for me, to both solidify my
wavering faith and ramify beyond it, to say more than I can say.

✤ ✤ ✤

In truth, though, what I crave at this point in my life is to speak more
clearly what it is that I believe. It is not that I am tired of poetic

truth, or that I feel it to be somehow weaker or less true than reason. The opposite is the case. Inspiration is to thought what grace is to faith: intrusive, transcendent, transformative, but also evanescent and, all too often, anomalous. A poem can leave its maker at once more deeply seized by existence and, in a profound way, alienated from it, for as the act of making ends—as the world that seemed to overbrim its boundaries becomes, once more, merely the world—it can be very difficult to retain any faith in that original moment of inspiration at all. The memory of that momentary blaze, in fact, and the art that issued from it, can become a reproach to the fireless life in which you find yourself most of the time. Grace is no different. (Artistic inspiration *is* sometimes an act of grace, though by no means always.) To experience grace is one thing; to integrate it into your life is quite another. What I crave now is that integration, some speech that is true to the transcendent nature of grace yet adequate to the hard reality in which daily faith operates. I crave, I suppose, the poetry *and* the prose of knowing.

✧ ✧ ✧

When I was young, twelve years old or so, I had an "experience" one morning in church. I put the word in quotes because, though the culture in which I was raised possessed definite language to explain what happened to me (I was filled with the Holy Spirit, I was saved), I no longer find that language accurate or helpful when thinking about how God manifests himself—or herself, or Godself, or whatever hopeless reflexive pronoun you want to use—in reality and individual lives. Also, I don't really remember the event. I remember that it happened, but it's in the half-wakeful, sedated way a man remembers a minor surgery. I remember being the subject of much adult awe and approbation, but even then the child those adults described, weeping and shaking and curled up tight in the church basement, was a stranger to me.

I grew up in a flat little sandblasted town in West Texas: pump-jacks and pickup trucks, cotton like grounded clouds, a dying strip, a lively dump, and above it all a huge blue and boundless void I never really noticed until I left, when it began to expand alarmingly inside of me. To call the place predominantly Christian is like calling the Sahara predominantly sand: I never met an actual unbeliever until my first day of college in Virginia, when a dauntingly hip prep-schooled freshman announced his atheism as casually as a culinary preference. Though I would presently embrace my own brand of bookish atheism—with, alas, a convert's fervor—just then I could not have been more shocked had that boy begun swiveling his head around and growling Aramaic.

The insularity that made my shock possible is, no doubt, precisely what made God possible—as a palpable reality, I mean, inclined to act on and in matter, to visit an unsuspecting soul like a blast of bad weather. That, according to my family, is what happened that day in the church when I rose during the call to be saved and, instead of heading toward the altar and the preacher's extended arms, fled the service entirely and ended up in the basement. What intensity seized me so utterly that I could not stay still? What love or judgment so overmastered me that I could not speak? Eventually my father found me, muttering incoherently, weeping—ecstatic. No one was in doubt about what had happened to me, nor did it matter that I myself had no idea. I had been visited just as Jacob or Mary was visited. I had been called, claimed.

It is somehow fitting that the most intense spiritual experience of my life should slip out of my memory like a dream (and that it should so resemble suffering, and that it should drive me straight out of the church that ostensibly prepared me for it). The moment means nothing to me now, and I'm inclined to rationalize it away: I grew up in a culture that encouraged conversions—*quiet* conversions, but still—in early adolescence. These were timed to coincide with a person's baptism, which for Baptists couldn't happen until you were old enough to understand the implications of what you were committing to. I was primed by the culture to experience *something*, and my own stifled imagination and primordial boredom conspired to answer that expectation with an outright rapture. In short, I faked it.

There are problems with this explanation. It's not really my nature, first of all: the theatricality, the willingness to be in an emotional spotlight, the unbottled expression of intense feelings—it all makes me feel a little creepy even thirty years on. It also seems unlikely that one would (or could) *forget* simulating an experience like this. The deliberation involved, the studied execution, all the excitement and concern of the other people—could all of that really just slip into oblivion?

There's another option, of course: it was real. Too real. Not in the way that some traumas are too real and thus buried within us, but in another, cellular sense, some complete being that I can't remember because I can't stand apart from it, can't find an "I" from which to see the self that, for a moment, I was. Or wasn't. If eternity touched you, if all the trappings of time and self were stripped away and you were all soul, if God "happened" to you—then isn't it possible that the experience could not be translated back into the land of pumpjacks and pickup trucks, the daily round wherein we use words like self and soul, revelation and conversion, as if we knew what those words meant? Maybe I didn't in fact "forget" it. Maybe it happened—and goes on happening—at the cellular level and means not nothing but everything to me. Maybe, like an atavistic impulse, I don't remember it, but it remembers me.

❖ ❖ ❖

If you return to the faith of your childhood after long wandering, people whose orientations are entirely secular will tend to dismiss or at least deprecate the action as having psychological motivations—motivations, it goes without saying, of which you are unconscious. As it happens, you have this suspicion yourself. It eats away at the intensity of the experience that made you proclaim, however quietly, your recovered faith, and soon you find yourself getting stalled in arguments between religion and science, theology and history, trying to nail down doctrine like some huge and much-torn tent in the wind.

In fact, there is no way to "return to the faith of your childhood," not really, not unless you've just woken from a decades-long and absolutely literal coma. Faith is not some half-remembered country into which you come like a long-exiled king, dispensing the old wisdom, casting out the radical, insurrectionist aspects of yourself by which you'd been betrayed. No. Life is not an error, even when it is. That is to say, whatever faith you emerge with at the end of your life is going to be not simply affected by that life but intimately dependent upon it, for faith in God is, in the deepest sense, faith in life—which means that even the staunchest life of faith is a life of great change. It follows that if you believe at fifty what you believed at fifteen, then you have not lived—or have denied the reality of your life.

To admit that there may be some psychological need informing your return to faith does not preclude or diminish the spiritual imperative, any more than acknowledging the chemical aspects of sexual attraction lessens the mystery of enduring human love. Faith cannot save you from the claims of reason, except insofar as it preserves and protects that wonderful, terrible time when reason, if only for a moment, lost its claim on you.

✤ ✤ ✤

On the radio I hear a famous novelist praising his father for enduring a long, difficult dying without ever "seeking relief in religion." It is clear from the son's description that the father was in absolute despair, and that as those cold waters closed over him he could find nothing to hold on to but his pride, and drowned clutching that nothing. This is to be admired? That we carry our despair stoically into death, that even the utmost anguish of our lives does not change us? How astonishing it is, the fierceness with which we cling to beliefs that have made us miserable, or beliefs that prove to be so obviously inadequate when extreme suffering—or great joy—comes. But the tension here is not simply between faith and the lack of it. A Christian who has lived with a steady but essentially shallow form of faith may find himself called to suffer the full human truth of God, which is the absence of God, may find himself finally confronted with the absolute emptiness of the cross. God calls to us at every moment, and God is life, *this* life. Radical change remains a possibility within us right up until our last breath. The greatest tragedy of human existence is not to live in time, in both senses of that phrase.

✢ ✢ ✢

I don't mean to suggest that the attitude of stoic acceptance is not at times a worthy one. I don't know what was going on in the mind of the novelist's father (the despair would seem to argue against stoic acceptance), but what was going on in the mind of the novelist himself is clear: it's the old fear of religion as crutch, Freudian wish fulfillment, a final refusal of life—which in order to *be* life must include a full awareness of death—rather than a final flowering of it. Some Christians love to point to (possibly apocryphal) anecdotes such as the one about Nietzsche, that idolater of pure power, going insane at the end of his life because he saw a horse being beaten; or Wallace Stevens, the great modern poet of unbelief, converting to Catholicism on his deathbed. But there are plenty of anecdotes to set against these: Freud's courage when suffering his final illness, Camus's staunch, independent humanism in the face of the chaos and depravity he both witnessed and imagined (". . . what we learn in time of pestilence: that there are more things to admire in men than to despise"—*The Plague*). There is not a trace of resignation or defeat in Camus. Indeed there is something in the stalwart, stubbornly humane nature of his metaphysical nihilism that constitutes a metaphysical belief. If it is true—and I think it is—that there is something lacking in this belief, that it seems more like one man's moral courage than a prescription for living, more a personal code than a universal creed, it is also true that all subsequent Christianity must pass through the "crucible of doubt" (as Dostoevsky, even earlier, called it) that such thinkers as Camus underwent.

✤ ✤ ✤

If God is a salve applied to unbearable psychic wounds, or a dream figure conjured out of memory and mortal terror, or an escape from a life that has become either too appalling or too banal to bear, then I have to admit: *it is not working for me.* Just when I think I've finally found some balance between active devotion and honest modern consciousness, all my old anxieties come pressuring up through the seams of me, and I am as volatile and paralyzed as ever. I can't tell which is worse, standing numb and apart from the world, wanting Being to burn me awake, or feeling that fire too acutely to crave anything other than escape into everydayness. What I do know is that the turn toward God has not lessened my anxieties, and I find myself continually falling back into wounds, wishes, terrors I thought I had risen beyond.

✤ ✤ ✤

Be careful. Be certain that your expressions of regret about your inability to rest in God do not have a tinge of self-satisfaction, even self-exaltation to them, that your complaints about your anxieties are not merely a manifestation of your dependence on them. There is nothing more difficult to outgrow than anxieties that have become useful to us, whether as explanations for a life that never quite finds its true force or direction, or as fuel for ambition, or as a kind of reflexive secular religion that, paradoxically, unites us with others in a shared sense of complete isolation: you feel at home in the world only by never feeling at home in the world.

※ ※ ※

It is this last complacency to which artists of our time are especially susceptible, precisely because it comes disguised as a lonely, heroic strength. Sometimes it truly is a strength: Giacometti, Beckett, Camus, Kafka. Yet it is a deep truth of being human—and, I would argue, a hint at the immortal Spirit who is forever tugging us toward him—that even our most imaginative discoveries are doomed to become mere stances and attitudes. In this sense, art does advance over time, though usually this advance involves a recovery of elements and ideas we thought we had left behind for good. This is true not only for those who follow in the wake of great accomplishments but also for those who themselves did the accomplishing. What belief could be more self-annihilating, could more effectively articulate its own insufficiency and thereby prophesy its own demise, than twentieth-century existentialism? To say that there is nothing beyond this world that we see, to make death the final authority of our lives, is to sow a seed of meaninglessness into that very insight. The four artists above all knew that, and made of that fatal knowledge a fierce, new, and necessary faith: the austere, "absurd" persistence of spirit in both Camus and Beckett; the terrible, disfiguring contingency that, in Giacometti's sculptures, takes on the look of fate. There is genuine heroism here, but there is also—faintly at first, but then more persistently, more damagingly—an awareness of heroism. (Only Kafka seems to fully feel his defeat: he is perhaps the most "spiritual" artist among this group, though he treasures his misery too much ever to be released from it.) This flaw—the artist's pride—is what made the achievement possible, but it is also the crack that slowly widens over time, not lessening the achievement, but humanizing it, relativizing it. Insights that once seemed immutable and universal begin to look a little more like temporal, individual visions—visions from which, inevitably, there comes a time to move forward.

✤ ✤ ✤

Christianity itself is this—temporal, relative—to some extent. To every age Christ dies anew and is resurrected within the imagination of man. This is why he could be a paragon of rationality for eighteenth-century England, a heroic figure of the imagination for the Romantics, an exemplar of existential courage for writers like Paul Tillich and Rudolf Bultmann. One truth, then, is that Christ is always being remade in the image of man, which means that his reality is always being deformed to fit human needs, or what humans perceive to be their needs. A deeper truth, though, one that scripture suggests when it speaks of the eternal Word being made specific flesh, is that there is no permutation of humanity in which Christ is not present. If every Bible is lost, if every church crumbles to dust, if the last believer in the last prayer opens her eyes and lets it all finally go, Christ will appear on this earth as calmly and casually as he appeared to the disciples walking to Emmaus after his death, who did not recognize this man to whom they had pledged their very lives; this man whom they had seen beaten, crucified, abandoned by God; this man who, after walking the dusty road with them, after sharing an ordinary meal and discussing the scriptures, had to vanish once more in order to make them see.

✤ ✤ ✤

When I think of the years when I had no faith, what I am struck by, first of all, is how little this lack disrupted my conscious life. I lived

not with God, nor with his absence, but in a mild abeyance of belief, drifting through the days on a tide of tiny vanities—a publication, a flirtation, a strong case made for some weak nihilism—nights
all adagios and alcohol as my mind tore luxuriously into itself. I can
see now how deeply God's absence affected my unconscious life, how
under me always there was this long fall that pride and fear and self-
love at once protected me from and subjected me to. Was the fall into
belief or into unbelief? Both. For if grace woke me to God's presence
in the world and in my heart, it also woke me to his absence. I never
truly felt the pain of unbelief until I began to believe.

✦ ✦ ✦

When I assented to the faith that was latent within me—and I phrase
it carefully, deliberately, for there was no white light, no ministering
or avenging angel that tore my life in two; rather it seemed as if the
tiniest seed of belief had finally flowered in me, or, more accurately,
as if I had happened upon some rare flower deep in the desert and
had known, though I was just then discovering it, that it had been
blooming impossibly year after parched year in me, surviving all
the seasons of my unbelief. *When I assented to the faith that was latent within me*, what struck me were the ways in which my evasions
and confusions, which I had mistaken for a strong sense of purpose,
had expressed themselves in my life: poem after poem about un-
named and unnameable absences, relationships so transparently per-
ishable they practically came with expiration dates on them, city
after city sacked of impressions and peremptorily abandoned, as if I
were some conquering army of insight seeing, I now see, nothing.
Perhaps it is never disbelief, which at least is active and conscious,
that destroys a person, but unacknowledged belief, or a need for belief so strong that it is continually and silently crucified on the crosses
of science, humanism, art, or (to name the thing that poisons all
these gifts of God) the overweening self.

✤ ✤ ✤

They do not happen now, the sandstorms of my childhood, when the western distance ochred and the square emptied, and long before the big wind hit, you could taste the dust on your tongue, could feel the earth under you—and even something in you—seem to loosen slightly. Soon tumbleweeds began to skip and nimble by, a dust devil flickered firelessly in the vacant lot across the street from our house, and birds began rocketing past with their wings shut as if they'd been flung. Worse than snow, worse than ice, a bad sandstorm shrinks the world to the slit of your eyes, lifting from the fields an inchoate, creaturely mass that claws at any exposed skin as if the dust remembered what it was, which is what you are—alive, alive— and sought return. They do not happen now, whether because of what we've learned or because the earth itself has changed. Yet I can close my eyes and see all the trees tugging at their roots as if to unfasten themselves from the earth. I can hear the long-gone howl, more awful for its being mute.

✤ ✤ ✤

Lord, I can approach you only by means of my consciousness, but consciousness can only approach you as an object, which you are not. I have no hope of experiencing you as I experience the world— directly, immediately—yet I want nothing more. Indeed, so great is my hunger for you—or is this evidence of your hunger for me?— that I seem to see you in the black flower mourners make beside a grave I do not know, in the embers' innards like a shining hive, in the bare abundance of a winter tree whose every limb is lit and fraught with snow. Lord, Lord, how bright the abyss inside that "seem."

SORROW'S FLOWER

Adele, who at nearly sixty years old finds that her faith has fallen away, tells me that it was love that first led her to God. Thirty-five years earlier, love for the man who would be her husband for most of her life seemed to crack open the world and her heart at the same time, seemed to fuse those latent, living energies into a single flame, the name of which, she knew, was God. There were careers and children. There were homes laid claim to and relinquished. There was something perhaps too usual for a love that had torn her so wholly open, but time takes the edge off of any experience, life means mostly waiting for life, or remembering it—right? She tells me all this—right up to the depressingly undramatic divorce—at a table outside in far West Texas, the country of my own heart.

✤ ✤ ✤

How can a love that seemed so fated fail so utterly? she wonders. How can a love that prompted me toward God become the very thing that kills my faith? Once it seemed love lit the world from within and made it take on a sacred radiance, but somehow that fire burned through everything and now I walk lost in this land of ash. If God by means of love became belief in my heart, became the faith by which I lived and loved in return, then what should I believe now that my love is dead? Or no, not dead; that would be easier. Actual death cuts life off at the quick of your soul, but there is yet the quick to tell you what life was, assure you *that* life was. You grieve the reality of your loss, not the loss of your reality. That former grief is awful, and may seem unendurable, but at least it is more productive, for it is grief that has lost but not renounced life, grief that still feels to the root the living reality of love because it feels so utterly that absence. All I feel is that the life I felt, the love that once scalded me toward God, was a lie.

✤ ✤ ✤

Christ is contingency, I tell her as we cross the railroad tracks and walk down the dusty main street of this little town that is not the town where I was raised, but both reassuringly and disconcertingly reminiscent of it: the ramshackle resiliency of the buildings around the square; Spanish rivering right next to rocklike English, the two fusing for a moment into a single dialect then splitting again; cowboys with creek-bed faces stepping determinedly out of the convenience store with sky in their eyes and twelve-packs in their arms. I have spent the past four weeks in solitude, working on these little prose fragments that seem to be the only thing I can sustain, trying day and night to "figure out" just what it is I believe, a mission made more urgent by the fact that I have recently been diagnosed with an incurable but unpredictable cancer. How strange it is to be back in this place, where visible distance is so much a part of things that things acquire a kind of space, as if even the single scrub cedar outside the window where I'm working held—in its precise little limbs, its assertive, seasonless green—the fact of its absence.

✤ ✤ ✤

Contingency. Meaning subject to chance, not absolute. Meaning uncertain, as reality, right down to the molecular level, is uncertain. As all of human life is uncertain. I suppose that to think of God in these terms might seem for some people deeply troubling (not to mention heretical), but I find it a comfort. It is akin to the notion of God entering and understanding—or understanding that there could be no understanding (*My God, my God, why hast thou forsaken me?*)—human suffering. If Christianity is going to mean anything at all for us now, then the humanity of God cannot be a half measure. He can't float over the chaos of pain and particles in which we're mired, and we can't think of him gliding among our ancestors like some shiny, sinless superhero. (The miracles, whatever one thinks of their veracity, didn't set Jesus off from his contemporaries as much as they seem to now; there were many healers, prophets, and the like wandering around the Middle East in the first century. And anyway, the miracles have a pro forma or applied quality even in the telling; often Jesus himself seeks to mute their effects, wants the people around him to place their faith in more common occurrences. And indeed, what is most moving and durable about Jesus are the moments of pure—at times even helpless: *My God, my God—* humanity.) No, God is given over to matter, the ultimate Uncertainty Principle. There's no release from reality, no "outside" or "beyond" from which some transforming touch might come. But what a relief it can be to befriend contingency, to meet God right here in the havoc of chance, to feel enduring love like a stroke of pure luck.

❖ ❖ ❖

Faith is not some hard, unchanging thing you cling to through the vicissitudes of life. Those who try to make it into this are destined to become brittle, shatterable creatures. Faith never grows harder, never so deviates from its nature and becomes actually destructive, than in the person who refuses to admit that faith is change. I don't mean simply that faith changes (though there is that). I mean that just as any sense of divinity that we have comes from the natural order of things—is in some ultimate sense *within* the natural order of things—so too faith is folded into change, is the mutable and messy process of our lives rather than any fixed, mental product. Those who cling to the latter are inevitably left with nothing to hold on to, or left holding on to some nothing into which they have poured the best parts of themselves. Omnipotent, eternal, omniscient—what in the world do these rotten words really mean? Are we able to imagine such attributes, much less perceive them? I don't think so. Christ is the only way toward knowledge of God, and Christ is contingency.

✦ ✦ ✦

The *only* way? Into my words, as into the things around me, seeps the silence that defeats them: if contingency equals absolute uncertainty and chance, then of course it makes no sense to assert it *as* an absolute. Better to say that contingency is the only way toward knowledge of God, and contingency, for Christians, is the essence of incarnation. And incarnation, as well as the possibilities for salvation within it, precedes Christ's presence in history, and exceeds all that is known by the term "Christianity":

> Into the instant's bliss never came one soul
> Whose soul was not possessed by Christ,
> Even in the eons Christ was not.
>
> And still: some who cry the name of Christ
> Live more remote from love
> Than some who cry to a void they cannot name.
>
> —AFTER DANTE

✦ ✦ ✦

I wouldn't want any of this to seem as if I'm blaming Adele for her suffering, or that I'm refusing to acknowledge the full impact of it. (*Christ is contingency*? What a ridiculous, riddling thing for me to have said to her at that moment. It was true, but the time and the context made it, in any ordinary human sense, false.) There is a sense in which love's truth *is* proved by its end, by what it becomes in us, and what we, by virtue of love, become. But love, like faith, occurs in the innermost recesses of a person's spirit, and we can see only inward in this regard, and not very clearly when it comes to that. And then, too, there can be great inner growth and strength in what seems, from the outside, like pure agony or destruction. In the tenderest spots of human experience, nothing is more offensive than intellectualized understanding. "Pain comes from the darkness / And we call it wisdom," writes Randall Jarrell. "It is pain."

✣ ✣ ✣

Sorrow is so woven through us, so much a part of our souls, or at least any understanding of our souls that we are able to attain, that every experience is dyed with its color. This is why, even in moments of joy, part of that joy is the seams of ore that are our sorrow. They burn darkly and beautifully in the midst of joy, and they make joy the complete experience that it is. But they still burn.

✣ ✣ ✣

And why this sorrow? Why its persistence, its involvement with all that is my soul? Childhood was difficult, and most of it remains inaccessible to me, but I was deeply loved. And I am capable of deep love now for the people in my life, for my work. I love the life that I have been granted in this deepening shadow of death. And it is not the prospect of my own death that sustains sorrow, for it preceded my sickness by many years, by all the years of my consciousness, in fact. And *that* is surely the reason right there—consciousness, which, at least as I have grown up understanding and developing it, is a setting apart from reality, when reality is the only possibility of God.

✤ ✤ ✤

For many people, God is simply a gauze applied to the wound of not knowing, when in fact that wound has bled into every part of the world, is bleeding now in a way that is life if we acknowledge it, death if we don't. Christ is contingency. Christ's life is *right now.*

I hear someone say on TV that one need only think of the million innocent children killed in the Holocaust to annihilate any notion of a benevolent God. True enough, I think, but that's a straw god, and not the real one who felt every one of those deaths as his own.

Felt? I listen to a radio segment about scientists measuring the radioactive decay after such large-scale catastrophes as September 11 or the 2003 tsunami in Indonesia. It turns out that nuclear decay, which is, if not a constant, as close to such a thing as we can get, inexplicably increases after these events. As if contingent matter echoed or shadowed or even shared our sufferings (and our joys?). As if creation itself cried out with us.

✤ ✤ ✤

Christ comes alive in the communion between people. When we are alone, even joy is, in a way, sorrow's flower: lovely, necessary, sustaining, but blooming in loneliness, rooted in grief. I'm not sure you can have communion with other people without these moments in which sorrow has opened in you, and for you; and I am pretty certain that without shared social devotion one's solitary experiences of

God wither into a form of withholding, spiritual stinginess, the light of Christ growing ever fainter in the glooms of the self.

❖ ❖ ❖

What this means is that even if you are socially shy and generally inarticulate about spiritual matters—and I say this as someone who finds casual social interactions often quite difficult and my own feelings about faith intractably mute—you must not swerve from the engagements God offers you. These will occur in the most unlikely places, and with people for whom your first instinct may be aversion. Dietrich Bonhoeffer says that Christ is always stronger in our brother's heart than in our own, which is to say, first, that we depend on others for our faith, and second, that the love of Christ is not something you can ever hoard. Human love catalyzes the love of Christ. And this explains why that love seems at once so forceful and so fugitive, and why, "while we speak of this, and yearn toward it," as Augustine says, "we barely touch it in a quick shudder of the heart."

❖ ❖ ❖

There is a kind of insistence on loneliness that is diabolical. It expunges the possibility of other people, of love in all its transfiguring forms, and thus of God. It does not follow, however, when one is freed from one's addiction to, or sentence of, loneliness, that loneliness "ends." But it becomes—even in love's afterimage, even when a love is taken from us—a condition in which God can be. Loneliness, when it passes through love, assumes an expansiveness and active capacity. "The body becomes an easy channel for the invisible," as Fanny Howe writes. "You may be lonely but are not empty."

❖ ❖ ❖

(How I pray for this condition for my wife, that she might know, when I am gone, this holy porousness, this presence that both stills and fulfills the ravages of absence, this gift beyond grief.)

✤ ✤ ✤

Last night we wondered whether people who do not have the love of God in them—or who have it but do not acknowledge it, or reject it—whether such people could fully feel human love. I was reading Hans Urs von Balthasar, who suggests that this is the case: God obstructs man, pursues man, haunts him with "a love that runs after him, pulls him out of the pit, casts aside his chains and places him in the freedom of divine and now even human love." *And now even human love.* For Balthasar, the man pursued by God may very well have loved another person, but not fully, not in the freedom of ultimate love, which scours the ego and urges one toward the spark of divinity within another person. It is those sparks that must unite; that is the only fire that time and change will not snuff out.

I have a complicated reaction to this. When my wife and I fell in love eight years ago, both of us—spontaneously, though we'd been away from any sort of organized religion for years—began praying together. The prayers were at once formal and improvisational, clear spirited but tentative, absolute but open ended. They were also, for all the whimsy of them (we would often laugh), deeply serious and, as my illness made clear when it came slashing through our lives, sustaining. Our passion had a religious element, which danger clarified and intensified. I don't think the human love preceded the divine love, exactly; as I have already said, I never experienced a conversion so much as an assent to a faith that had long been latent within me. But it was human love that reawakened divine love. Put another way, it was pure contingency that caught fire in our lives, and it was Christ whom we found—together, and his presence dependent upon our being together—burning there. I can't speak for other people. I only know that I did not know what love was until I encountered one that kept opening and opening and opening. And until I acknowledged that what that love was opening onto, and into, was God.

✣ ✣ ✣

But reflect, daughters, that He doesn't want you to hold on to anything, for if you avoid doing so you will be able to enjoy the favors we are speaking of. Whether you have little or much, He wants everything for Himself; and in conformity with what you know you have given, you will receive greater or lesser favors.

—TERESA OF AVILA

There is much in this passage that clearly anchors it in, and limits it to, an earlier time and consciousness—the uncomplicated personification of God ("he wants"), the presentation of God as a kind of endlessly craving and endlessly jealous father figure, and (worst of all) the assumption that there is a direct link between the quality of your prayers and offerings and the quality of God's response: what you give is what you get. But there is also a deep truth in the passage that transcends all of this. In any true love—a mother's for her child, a husband's for his wife, a friend's for a friend—there is an excess energy that always wants to be in motion. Moreover, it seems to move not simply from one person to another but through them, toward something else. ("All I know now / is the more he loved me the more I loved the world."—Spencer Reece) This is why we can be so baffled and overwhelmed by such love (and I don't mean merely when we fall in love; in fact, I'm talking more of other, more durable relationships): it wants to be more than it is; it cries out inside of us to make it more than it is. And what it is crying out for, finally, is its essence and origin: God. Love, which awakens our souls and to which we cling like the splendid mortal creatures that we are, asks us to let it go, to let it be more than it is if it is *only* us. To manage this highest form of loving does not mean that we will be showered with earthly delights or somehow be spared awful human suffering. But for as long as we can live in this sacred space of receiving and releasing, and can learn to speak and be love's fluency, then the greater love that is God brings a continuous and enlarging air into our existence. We feel love leave us in unthreatening ways. We feel it reenter us at once more truly and more strange, like a simple kiss that has a bite of starlight to it.

✦ ✦ ✦

At once more truly and more strange. I used the phrase before I remembered the source. And an ironic source it is. Here is Wallace Stevens's "Tea at the Palaz of Hoon":

Not less because in purple I descended
The western day through what you called
The loneliest air, not less was I myself.

What was the ointment sprinkled on my beard?
What were the hymns that buzzed beside my ears?
What was the sea whose tide swept through me there?

Out of my mind the golden ointment rained,
And my ears made the blowing hymns they heard.
I was myself the compass of that sea:

I was the world in which I walked, and what I saw
Or heard or felt came not but from myself;
And there I found myself more truly and more strange.

Beautiful poem, fatal belief. That you are the origin of everything, that the self is its own world, its own god. But, as is often the case, you can't quite tell if Stevens really believes what the music is making him say: that "you" in line two, and her (let's make it a her) description of his regal aloofness as lonely, introduce another mind and other needs into the poem. The music moves right past them, but they are there. Like the title, lovely but also slightly ridiculous, the "you" is a hitch in an otherwise perfect, and perfectly self-enclosed, song. And the song is better, and truer, for it.

❖ ❖ ❖

How many loves fail because, in an unconscious effort to make our weaknesses more strong, we link with others precisely at those points? How many women who are not mothers spend years mothering some mysteriously wounded man? How many apparently strong and successful men seek out love like a kind of topical balm they can apply to their wounded bodies and egos when they have withdrawn from combat? Herein lies the great difference between divine weakness and human weakness, the wounds of Christ and the wounds of man. Two human weaknesses only intensify each other. But human weakness plus Christ's weakness equals a supernatural strength.

❖ ❖ ❖

Not long after I first learned that I was sick, in the dim time of travel, multiple doctors, and endless tests, when it seemed that I might be in danger of dying very soon, I began to meet every Friday afternoon with the pastor at the church just around the corner from where my wife and I lived. I think that he, like anyone whose faith is healthy, actively craved instances in which that faith might be tested. So we argued for an hour every Friday, though that verb is completely wrong for the complex, respectful, difficult interactions we had. Nothing was ever settled. In fact my friend—for we became close friends—seemed to me mulishly orthodox at times, just as I seemed to him, I know, either boneheadedly literal when I focused on scripture or woozily mystical when I didn't. And yet those hours and the time afterward, when, strangely enough, I didn't so much think about all that we had discussed as feel myself *freed* from such thoughts, are among the happiest hours of my life. Grief was not suspended or banished, but entered and answered. Answered not by theology, and not by my own attempts to imaginatively circumvent theology, but by the depth and integrity and essential innocence of the communion occurring between two people.

✤ ✤ ✤

William James said that our inner lives are fluid and restless and always in transition, and that our experience "lives in the transitions." This seems to me true. It is why every single expression of faith is provisional—because life carries us always forward to a place where the faith we'd fought so hard to articulate to ourselves must now be reformulated, and because faith in God is, finally, faith in change.

Still, it can be easy to understand and apply this idea too bluntly, easy to turn it into the kind of inhuman truth that eats up ordinary lives, and ordinary life. For it is only a short step from saying that our experience "lives in the transitions" to saying that one ought to seek out and even provoke these transitions: if I am closest to God when I am most in crisis, then bring on the whirlwind; if I am most alive when love is beginning or ending, then let this marriage die, let this affair take flame, let me let myself go. Thus do many believers lurch from one extreme of belief to another, thus do many men and women enter a relationship with dead stars in their eyes.

The truth in James's idea inheres in that "always." If our inner lives are always in transition, then our goal should be to acquire and refine a consciousness that is capable of registering the most minute changes in sensation, feeling, faith, self. Unless we become aware of the transitions that are occurring all the time within us, unless we learn to let experience play upon our inner lives as on a finely tuned instrument, we will try to manufacture inner intensity from the outside, we will bang our very bones to roust our own souls. We crave radical ruptures when we have allowed the nerves of our inner lives to go numb. But after those ruptures—the excitement or the tragedy, the pleasure or the pain—the mind returns to what it was, the soul quicksilvers off from the pierce of experience, and the kingdom of boredom, which could be the kingdom of God, begins the clock-tick toward its next collapse.

✤ ✤ ✤

Be careful what you wish for, be ready for what you crave:

> If I ask you, angel, will you come and lead
> This ache to speech, or carry me, like a child,
> To riot?
>   —EDGAR BOWERS, FROM "AUTUMN SHADE"

✤ ✤ ✤

A friend once told me that she could wake up a Christian and go to bed an atheist, that every day was this vertiginous inward to-and-fro with God. I found this both heartening and depressing: heartening in that if she experiences this spiritual vertigo, she whose life seems to me so lit by Christ, then I certainly needn't be ashamed of my own confusions; depressing in that if *she* experiences this, then there's no escape from it, ever. If I am honest with myself, I feel mostly the distance, and this incessant, desperate, and (I have to believe) holy hunger to bridge it. Experience lives in the transitions. We feel ourselves alive in the anxiety of being alive. We feel God in the coming and going of God—or no, the coming and going of consciousness (God is constant). We are left with these fugitive instants of apprehension, in both senses of that word, which is one reason why poetry, which is designed not simply to arrest these instants but to integrate them into life, can be such a powerful aid to faith.

✢ ✢ ✢

MEDITATION ON A GRAPEFRUIT

To wake when all is possible
before the agitations of the day
have gripped you
            To come to the kitchen
and peel a little basketball
for breakfast
            To tear the husk
like cotton padding   a cloud of oil
misting out of its pinprick pores
clean and sharp as pepper
                  To ease
each pale pink section out of its case
so carefully   without breaking
a single pearly cell
            To slide each piece
into a cold blue china bowl
the juice pooling   until the whole
fruit is divided from its skin
and only then to eat

so sweet
        a discipline
precisely pointless   a devout
involvement of the hands and senses
a pause   a little emptiness

each year harder to live within
each year harder to live without
         —CRAIG ARNOLD

❖ ❖ ❖

Love does not die without our assent, though often (usually) that assent has been given unconsciously long before we come to give it consciously. Love is not only given by God, it is sustained by him. There is a constant interplay between divine and human love. Human love has an end, which is God, who makes it endless.

❖ ❖ ❖

What you must realize, what you must even come to praise, is the fact that there is no *right way* that is going to become apparent to you once and for all. The most blinding illumination that strikes and perhaps radically changes your life will be so attenuated and obscured by doubts and dailiness that you may one day come to suspect the truth of that moment at all. The calling that seemed so clear will be lost in echoes of questionings and indecision; the church that seemed to save you will fester with egos, complacencies, banalities; the deepest love of your life will work itself like a thorn in your heart until all you can think of is plucking it out. Wisdom is accepting the truth of this. Courage is persisting with life in spite of it. And faith is finding yourself, in the deepest part of your soul, in the very heart of who you are, moved to praise it.

✧ ✧ ✧

Several years have passed since I wrote the first words of this chapter. I have been in and out of treatment, in and out of the hospital. I have had bones die and bowels fail; joints lock in my face and arms and legs, so that I could not eat, could not walk. I have filled my body with mingled mouse and human antibodies, cutting-edge small molecules, old-school chemotherapies eating into me like animate acids. I have passed through pain I could never have imagined, pain that seemed to incinerate all my thoughts of God and to leave me sitting there in the ashes, alone. I have been isolated even from my wife, though her love was constant, as was mine. I have come back, for now, even hungrier for God, for *Christ*, for all the difficult bliss of this life I have been given. But there is great weariness too. And fear. And fury.

I haven't been in contact with Adele since the morning I left Texas, when she called just as I was heading out the door. There was a moment of silence before we stumbled all over each other trying to convey how much our tentative and half-candid time together had meant to each of us, the spark of spirit that (though we didn't say so) burned there. We didn't exchange e-mails. We didn't promise to stay in touch. It was a moment, and we acknowledged it as such, before letting it sink back into our fluid and restless inner lives to do its work there.

✧ ✧ ✧

My sorrow's flower was so small a joy
It took a winter seeing to see it as such.
Numb, unsteady, stunned at all the evidence

Of winter's one imperative to destroy,
I looked up, and saw the bare abundance
Of a tree whose every limb was lit and fraught with snow.
What I was seeing then I did not quite know
But knew that one mite more would have been too much.

TENDER INTERIOR

In my early twenties I found myself reduced to living in a twenty-five-foot trailer in a tiny, dying town in far West Texas. There was a certain unresonant symmetry to the experience, as I had lived in the trailer as an infant, along with my older brother and our almost-infant parents. By the time of this second residence, the trailer was in my grandmother's backyard, where my great-grandmother had lived for thirty years until her death, in 1990. My grandmother's sister—Aunt Sissy, to me—a gentle, whiskery woman with failing health and an obvious but undiagnosed lifelong mental deficiency, also lived in the "big house," which was a small house with six shadowy rooms, a million immaculate nooks, and museum stillnesses. I read and wrote all day, then sat with my grandmother and aunt in the evenings to pass the time.

Or to recover the time. After college and knocking about in various countries, after falling away from my childhood faith and transferring that entire searching intensity onto literature, it seemed to me that though I was home again, I would never be able to *be* at home again. It's an old story, as is the lost world and wisdom the prodigal discovers beyond his own ambitions and self-assurance. Out of politeness and boredom, I began asking questions about my family's past. I ended up arranging my days, my thoughts, and my work around the world that emerged from those conversations: the mythic migration from South Carolina to Texas in the dust bowl; the years spent sharecropping; my grandmother's many miscarriages; my aunt's thirty years of waitressing at a cowboy café just off the interstate.

God was almost instinctive in them, so woven into the textures of their lives that even their daily chores, accompanied by hymns hummed under their breath, had an air of easy devotion. I looked down on that unanguished faith at the time, but now, after living with my own vertiginous intensities for all these years, that quiet constancy is a disposition to which I aspire.

Not that there wasn't, in the end, anguish for them. Sissy died with my grandmother and me leaning over her hospital bed, as we had done for days and nights since she had suffered a heart attack. She was not conscious during that time, but just before the end, when my grandmother and I were bent above her inert and unresponsive body to tell her that we were there, that we loved her, that God was there and loved her (I didn't say this), she rose up, took each one of us in her trembling arms ("Praise the Lord," said the nurse in awe), and then, without a word or even any clear indication that she was conscious, let us go. Later that day, she died.

My grandmother was destroyed. Not by grief—she'd had too much of it in her life to be undone by this point—but by the strain of taking care of Sissy during the last year of her life, and then the intense ten days or so when Sissy was hospitalized. My grandmother's own heart began aching ominously just as Sissy's finally stopped, and though my grandmother had yet a month of modern medicine to endure, she never made it out of the hospital. And so it was that I found myself, just weeks after Sissy's last improbable act, leaning over another hospital bed, trying to understand another dying woman's desperate gestures. I asked my grandmother if she was cold, and she shook her head no. I asked if she was thirsty, and she shook her head no. Finally I asked—I did not want to—if she was scared, and her eyes widened even farther and she began to shake terribly as she nodded yes and tried to form words around her breathing tube: yes, yes, yes. I suppose I don't know definitively whether she was afraid of dying or of further pain—she had been through so much by that time—but all my instincts argue for the former. I could see a pure spiritual terror in her eyes. I can see it now.

The last words of Gerard Manley Hopkins, a poet and priest who died of typhoid at the age of forty-five, are striking: "I am so happy. I am so happy. I loved my life." How desperately we, the living, want to believe in this possibility: that death could be filled with promise, that the pain of leaving and separation could be, if not a foretaste of joy, then at least not meaningless. Forget religion. Even atheists want to die well, or want those they love to die well, which has to mean more than simply a quiet resignation to complete annihilation. That is merely a polite nihilism. No, to die well, even for the religious, is to accept not only our own terror and sadness but the terrible holes we leave in the lives of others; at the same time, to die well, even for the atheist, is to believe that there is some way of dying *into* life rather than simply away from it, some form of survival that love makes possible. I don't mean by survival merely persisting in the memory of others. I mean something deeper and more durable. If quantum entanglement is true, if related particles react in similar or opposite ways even when separated by tremendous distances, then it is obvious that the whole world is alive and communicating in ways we do not fully understand. And we are part of that life, part of that communication— even as, maybe even *especially* as, our atoms begin the long dispersal we call death.

Hopkins's last words are striking to me not only because it's rare and heartening to witness someone expressing joy at an occasion for grief. No, it's the last sentence that gets me—*I loved my life.* Hopkins was a religious person; he believed in an afterlife. But he seems to have experienced something more complicated than the typical (and, I feel, pernicious) religious sentiment of being happy to be "going to a better place"; the last sentence seems offered as an explanation for the first two: he is happy at the moment of death because he loved his life. On the face of it, this makes no sense: if he loved his life so much, how could he be happy that it was ending so early? The answer, I think, lies in that dynamic of life and death that I've just described, that capacity of dying into the life that one has loved rather than falling irrevocably away from it.

As it happens, I have been close to death myself lately. The cancer I have lived with for seven years has of late become aggressive, and in the past year I have on many nights lain awake in hospital beds and wondered what last gesture or insight I might manage or be granted, have felt despair rising like a palpable and impenetrable liquid in my room. Though I have not yet known that knife-edge of time—and timelessness—that Hopkins and my aunt Sissy and my grandmother all knew, I have been close enough, and deranged by pain enough, to conclude that one is not always responsible for one's last acts, nor are they always worth interpretation. Sissy seemed to reach out of the shell of herself for one last loving touch of life. My grandmother shook as if the scream she couldn't release ricocheted around inside of her. I treasure the memory of Sissy, flinch from that image of my grandmother. Yet I don't feel that one died well and the other badly, that one received the grace that the other either denied or was refused. Hopkins's last words are about life, all of life, and its ultimate relation to death. That they occurred at the last moment of his own life makes them more poignant and powerful, but that he had the wherewithal to speak them is chance.

What does faith mean, finally, at this late date? I often feel that it means no more than, and no less than, faith in life—in the ongoingness of it, the indestructibility, some atom-by-atom intelligence that is and isn't us, some day-by-day and death-by-death persistence insisting on a more-than-human hope, some tender and terrible energy that is, for those with the eyes to see it, love. My grandmother, who was in the world too utterly to be "conscious" of it, whose spirit poured and pours over the cracked land of her family like a saving rain, exemplified this energy, and I feel that to be faithful *to her*, faithful to this person that I loved as much as I have ever loved anyone, I must believe in the scope and momentum of her life, not the awful and anomalous instant of her death. In truth, it is not difficult at all. Nor is the other belief—or instinct, really—that occurs simultaneously: that her every tear was wiped away, that God looked her out of pain, that in the blink of an eye the world opened its tenderest interiors, and let her in.

GOD'S TRUTH IS LIFE

When I was twenty years old I spent an afternoon with Howard Nemerov. He was the first "famous" poet I had ever met, though I would later learn that he was deeply embittered by what he perceived to be a lack of respect from critics and other poets. (I once heard Thom Gunn call him a "zombie.") My chief memories are of his great eagerness to nail down the time and place for his midday martini, his reciting "Animula" when I told him I loved Eliot, and his asking me at one point—with what I now realize was great patience and kindness—what I was going to do when I graduated from college later that year. I had no plans, no ambitions clear enough to recognize as such, no interest in any of the things that my classmates were hurtling toward. Poetry was what I spent more and more of my time working on, though I found that vaguely embarrassing, even when revealing it to a real poet, as I did. Equivocations spilled out of me then, how poetry was all right as long as one didn't take it too seriously, as long as one didn't throw one's whole life into it. He set down his martini and looked at me for a long moment—I feel the gaze now—then looked away.

✤ ✤ ✤

The irony is that for the next two decades I would be so consumed with poetry that I would damn near forget the world. One must have devotion to be an artist, and there's no way of minimizing its cost. But still, just as in religious contexts, there is a kind of devotion that is, at its heart, escape.

> These poems, these poems,
> these poems, she said, are poems
> with no love in them. These are the poems of a man
> who would leave his wife and child because
> they made noise in his study. These are the poems
> of a man who would murder his mother to claim
> the inheritance. These are the poems of a man
> like Plato, she said, meaning something I did not
> comprehend but which nevertheless
> offended me. These are the poems of a man
> who would rather sleep with himself than with women,
> she said. These are the poems of a man
> with eyes like a drawknife, with hands like a pickpocket's
> hands, woven of water and logic
> and hunger, with no strand of love in them. These
> poems are as heartless as birdsong, as unmeant
> as elm leaves, which if they love love only
> the wide blue sky and the air and the idea
> of elm leaves. Self-love is an ending, she said,
> and not a beginning. Love means love
> of the thing sung, not of the song or the singing.
> These poems, she said. . . .
>   You are, he said,
> beautiful.
>   That is not love, she said rightly.
>   —"THESE POEMS, SHE SAID"

For years I carried this poem by the Canadian poet Robert Bring-hurst in my mind like a totem. I loved its quality of highly dramatized speech, the sense it gives that we might actually say to each other things like "these poems are as heartless as birdsong, as unmeant as elm leaves." I loved the mix of intellect and sensuousness, abstraction and concretion, passion and intelligence. Most of all, though, I loved *what* the poem was saying, and how it seemed to so perfectly dramatize tensions I felt in my life every day: between art and the people I loved, between art and my responsibilities in the world and to other people, between art and my hunger for an experience of life that was immediate, unmediated, *mine*. As W. B. Yeats put it more than a hundred years ago, had such an experience ever actually happened, "I might have thrown poor words away / and been content to live."

If you've never been consumed by an art, it might seem strange to think of it in these terms—as an antithesis to life, almost, or at least as a kind of parasite. But the fact is, art can compromise, even in some way neutralize, the very experience on which it depends. If to be an artist is to be someone upon whom nothing is lost, as Henry James said, then it follows that to be an artist is to be in some permanent sense professionally detached. An artist is conscious of always standing apart from life, and one of the results of this can be that you begin to feel most intensely what you have *failed* to feel: a certain emotional reserve in one's life becomes a source of great power in one's work. That poem by Bringhurst serves as both an example of this power—it carries a strong emotional charge even as it articulates emotional distance—and a reprimand to it, labeling all that supposed artistic discipline, all that self-exonerating crap about being "a person upon whom nothing is lost," as merely a species of self-love.

Given all this, it's not surprising that some religious poets have felt a difficult tension between their devotion to art and their devotion to God. Hopkins actually renounced poetry for a number of years. His reason was that poetry wasn't consistent with the seriousness of his vocation, but you don't need to read much of Hopkins to realize that the real reason was that the intensity of his creative experiences competed with the intensity of his religious experiences, and he felt himself presented with a stark choice. Then there's George Herbert. He was also a priest, an Anglican, though not until late in his life, after he had served two terms in Parliament. Though Herbert sometimes linked poetry to God and experienced grace through words, he was conscious of some secular element at the very heart of making art, some necessary imaginative flair in himself that needed to be subdued, or at least tidied up and made fit for sacrifice:

> Farewell, sweet phrases, lovely metaphors:
> But will ye leave me thus? When ye before
> Of stews and brothels onely knew the doores,
> Then did I wash you with my tears, and more,
> Brought you to church well drest and clad:
> My God must have my best, ev'n all I had.
> —FROM "THE FORERUNNERS"

I have always responded deeply to these two poets—I don't know that any poet, of any time, is more companionable to me than Herbert ("Sorrow was all my soul; I scarce believed, / Till grief did tell me roundly, that I lived"). But I've never experienced the tension between poetry and God in quite the same terms. The Scottish runner Eric Liddell, whose story is told in the movie *Chariots of Fire*, once explained why he couldn't give up running—not yet, at any rate—to be a missionary in China: "I believe that God made me for a purpose," Liddell said, "but he also made me fast, and when I run I feel his pleasure . . . To give up running would be to hold him in contempt." I like this notion: God doesn't give a gift without giving an obligation to use it. *How* one uses it, though—that's where things get complicated.

And the fact is, during all those years when that Bringhurst poem was my own little private anthem, when I practiced absence like a kind of discipline, moving forty times in fifteen years, owning nothing that wouldn't fit in the trunk of my car, distancing myself from my family, my home, my very self in order to feel these energies in my art—during all that time, I did not think of God. I mean, I *thought* of God, but only as a kind of intellectual stopgap, an ultimate synonym for ultimate absence, some vague and almost purely rhetorical gesture that signaled little more than a failure of both words and intellect. In retrospect it seems to me obvious what was going on, what ultimate insight was lacking from, and therefore clouding and diminishing, every sight, what hunger ruined my taste, even as it increased my desire, for the world. "Who here is the finished man / whose hands know only what is gone?" I wrote at the time in a poem I've never published. "All night he holds it as he can, / his losses lost again in song."

During one of those years I lived in Prague. I was living with someone at the time. Unlike some of the relationships I was in during those years, this one was intimate, long lasting, and remains part of the bedrock of my consciousness. We lived in one of those grim, gray apartment blocks that surround every Eastern European city, but we lived on the top floor, so we had a tremendous view of Prague for about thirty dollars a month. (This was the year after the Velvet Revolution, when tourists were scarce and prices were still low.) One day when I was studying Czech at the kitchen table and my girlfriend was taking a bath in the other room, a falcon landed on the windowsill—maybe three feet from me. A decade later, after that bedrock in my brain had ruptured in ways I realize are never quite going to heal, I wrote a poem called "Poštolka," which in Czech means falcon or, more accurately, kestrel:

When I was learning words
And you were in the bath
There was a flurry of small birds
And in the aftermath

Of all that panicked flight,
As if the red dusk willed
A concentration of its light,
A falcon on the sill.

It scanned the orchard's bowers,
Then pane by pane it eyed
The stories facing ours
But never looked inside.

I called you in to see.
And when you'd steamed the room
And naked next to me
Stood dripping, as a bloom

Of blood formed in your cheek
And slowly seemed to melt
I could almost speak
The love I almost felt.

Wish for something, you said.
A shiver pricked my spine.
The falcon turned its head
And locked its eyes on mine

And for a long moment I'm still in
I wished and wished and wished
The moment would not end.
And just like that it vanished.

This is a love poem by a person who is incapable of love. It's a
rapture of time by someone who never quite enters it, a celebration

of life by a man whose mind is tuned only to elegies. It is also, I've come to think, in a peculiar and very modern sense, a devotional poem, or at least an early unconscious attempt at one, though God is nowhere in it. That's what makes it modern.

✣ ✣ ✣

I once believed in some notion of a pure ambition, which I defined as an ambition for the work rather than for oneself. But now? If a poet's ambition were truly for the work and nothing else, he would write under a pseudonym, which would not only preserve that pure space of making but free him from the distractions of trying to forge a name for himself in the world. No, all ambition has the reek of disease about it, the relentless smell of the self—except for that terrible, blissful feeling at the heart of creation itself, when all thought of your name is obliterated and all you want is the poem, to be the means wherein something of reality, perhaps even something of eternity, realizes itself. That is noble ambition. But all that comes after—the need for approval, publication, self-promotion—isn't this what usually goes under the name of "ambition"? The effort is to make ourselves more real to ourselves, to feel that we *have* selves, though the deepest moments of creation tell us that, in some fundamental way, we don't. (*Souls* are what those moments reveal, which are both inside and outside, both us and other.) So long as your ambition is to stamp your existence upon existence, your nature on nature, then your ambition is corrupt and you are pursuing a ghost.

✣ ✣ ✣

Still, there is *something* that any artist is in pursuit of, and is answerable to, some nexus of one's being, one's material, and Being itself. Inspiration is when these three things collide—or collude. The work that emerges from this crisis of consciousness may be judged a failure or a success by the world, and that judgment will still sting or flatter your vanity. But it cannot speak to this crisis in which, for which, and of which the work was made. For any artist alert to his own soul, this crisis is the only call that matters. I know no name for it besides God, but people have other names, or no names.

❖ ❖ ❖

This truth places the artist under the most severe pressure: if that original call, that crisis of consciousness, either has not been truly heard or has not been answered with everything that is in you, then even the loudest clamors of approval will be tainted and the wounds of rejection salted with your implacable self-knowledge. An artist who loses this internal arbiter is an artist who can no longer hear the call that first came to him.

❖ ❖ ❖

These days I am impatient with poetry that is not steeped in, marred and transfigured by, the world. By that I don't necessarily mean poetry that has some obvious social concern or is meticulous with its descriptions, but a poetry in which you can feel that the imagination of the poet has been both charged and chastened by a full encounter with the world and other lives. A poet like Robert Lowell, who had such a tremendous imagination for language but so little for other people, means less and less to me as the years pass. On the other hand, a poet like Gwendolyn Brooks, with her saturation of rough, real Bronzeville, or Lorine Niedecker, with her "full foamy folk" of eastern Wisconsin—

I worked the print shop
right down among em

the folk from whom all poetry flows
and dreadfully much else

—these poets seem to be throwing me lifelines from their graves.

✣ ✣ ✣

The Lutheran pastor and theologian Dietrich Bonhoeffer, a radiant moral presence amid the murderous twentieth century, was safe in the United States when Hitler's intentions began to be made clear. He could have stayed here, could have assumed a prestigious post at Union Theological Seminary and spent his life as a comfortable and influential public intellectual. But the decision was not all that difficult for him: he went back to a disintegrating and dangerous Germany because, as he said, if he did not suffer his country's destruction, he could not credibly participate in its restoration. He went back because, as he had written earlier, "Only the obedient believe. If we are to believe, we must obey a concrete command."

For all the modern talk about keeping an author's work and life separate, all the schoolroom injunctions against mistaking art for autobiography, there are some works that life electrifies with meaning, some sayings only action authenticates. The charge is not always a positive one: Sylvia Plath's late poems are so disturbing and powerful precisely because she committed the awful act around which they danced. The act is not always a willful one: the Hungarian poet Miklós Radnóti, after a long forced march with hundreds of other doomed men, was killed by the Nazis and dumped into a mass grave in 1944. After the war, when his body was exhumed and identified, his wife discovered in his coat pocket a small notebook filled with poems he had written during his last days. Prophetic, apocalyptic, and yet brutally specific, the poems are at once unflinching and uncanny. "The reader approaches these with a certain veneration," writes the poet and translator George Szirtes, "as though they were more than poems. Slowly, everything assumes a mythic shape and the life embraces the oeuvre so comprehensively that the one disappears in the other."

Bonhoeffer was a theologian, not an artist (though he did have a gift for the kind of encompassing compression and lucid paradox that are hallmarks of poetry), but the effect is the same:

> The important thing today is that we should be able to discern from the fragment of our life how the whole was arranged and planned, and what material it consists of.

> For acquired knowledge cannot be divorced from the existence in which it is acquired. The only man who has the right to say that he is justified by grace alone is the man who has left all to follow Christ.

> Every real action is of such a kind that no one other than oneself can do it.

It hardly matters whether or not one "agrees" with any of this. The words have an authenticity and authority beyond mere intellectual assertion: they burn with the brave and uncompromising life—and death—that lie behind them.

Dietrich Bonhoeffer was executed at the Flossenbürg concentration camp on April 9, 1945.

❖ ❖ ❖

Bonhoeffer, after being in prison for a year, still another hard year away from his execution, forging long letters to his friend Eberhard Bethge out of his strong faith, his anxiety, his longing for his fiancée, and terror over the nightly bombings: "There are things more important than self-knowledge." Yes. An artist who believes this is an artist of faith, even if the faith contains no god.

⁂

> I often ask myself why a "Christian instinct" often draws me more to the religionless people than to the religious, by which I don't in the least mean with any evangelizing intention, but, I might almost say, "in brotherhood."
>
> —DIETRICH BONHOEFFER

⁂

Reading Bonhoeffer makes me realize again how small our points of contact with life can be, perhaps even necessarily *are*, when our truest self finds its emotional and intellectual expression. With all that is going on around Bonhoeffer, and with all the people in his life (he wrote letters to many other people and had close relationships with other prisoners), it is only in the letters to Bethge that his thought really sparks and finds focus. Life is *always* a question of intensity, and intensity is always a matter of focus. Contemporary despair is to feel the multiplicity of existence with no possibility for expression or release of one's particular being. I fear sometimes that we are evolving in such a way that the possibilities for these small but intense points of intimacy and expression—poetry, for instance—are not simply vanishing but are becoming no longer felt as necessary pressures.

⁂

Our minds are constantly trying to bring God down to our level rather than letting him lift us into levels of which we were not previously capable. This is as true in life as it is in art. Thus we love within the lines that experience has drawn for us, we create out of impulses that are familiar and, if we were honest with ourselves, exhausted. What might it mean to be drawn into meanings that, in some profound and necessary sense, shatter us? This is what it means to love. This is what it *should* mean to write one more poem. The inner and outer urgency of it, the mysterious and confused agency of it. All love abhors habit, and poetry is a species of love.

✤ ✤ ✤

Art needs some ultimate concern, to use Paul Tillich's phrase. As belief in God waned among late-nineteenth- and early-twentieth-century artists, death became their ultimate concern. Dickinson, Stevens, Beckett, Camus—these are the great devotional poets of death. Postmodernism sought to eliminate death in the frenzy of the instant, to deflect it with irony and hard-edged surfaces in which, because nothing was valued more than anything else, nothing was subject to ultimate confirmation or denial. This was a retreat from the cold eye cast on death by the modernists, and the art of postmodernism is, as a direct consequence, less urgent. I suspect that the only possible development now is to begin finding a way to once more imagine ourselves into and out of death, though I also feel quite certain that the old religious palliatives, at least those related to the Christian idea of heaven, are inadequate.

✤ ✤ ✤

The three living novelists whose work means most to me are Cormac McCarthy (*Blood Meridian*), Fanny Howe (*Indivisible*), and Marilynne Robinson (*Housekeeping* and *Gilead*). All these writers seem to me to have not only the linguistic and metaphorical capacities of great poets (Howe is a poet) but also genuine visionary feeling. My own predispositions have everything to do with my preference, of course: I *believe* in visionary feeling and experience, and in the capacity of art to realize those things. I also believe that visionary art is a higher achievement than art that merely concerns itself with the world that is right in front of us. Thus I don't respond as deeply to William Carlos Williams as I do to T. S. Eliot, and I much prefer Wallace Stevens (the earlier work) to, say, Elizabeth Bishop. (To read "Sunday Morning" as it apparently asks to be read, to take its statements about reality and transcendence at face value, is to misread—to *under*-read—that poem. Its massive organ music and formal grandeur are not simply aiming at transcendence, they are claiming it.) Successful visionary art is a rare thing, and too much of it will leave one not simply blunted to its effects but also craving art that's deeply attached to this world and nothing else. This latter category includes most of the art in existence—even much art that seems to be religious.

❖ ❖ ❖

Some poets—surprisingly few—have a very particular gift for making a thing at once shine forth in its "thingness" and ramify beyond its own dimensions. Norman MacCaig: "Straws like tame lightnings lie about the grass / And hang zigzag on hedges." Or: "The black cow is two native carriers / Bringing its belly home, slung from a pole." What happens here is not "the extraordinary discovered within the ordinary," a cliché of poetic perception. What happens is some mysterious resonance between thing and language, mind and matter, that reveals—and it does feel like revelation—a reality beyond the one we ordinarily see. Contemporary physicists talk about something called "quantum weirdness," which refers to the fact that an observed particle behaves very differently from one that is unobserved. An observed particle passed through a screen will always go through one hole. A particle that is unobserved but mechanically monitored will pass through multiple holes at the same time. What this suggests is that what we call reality is conditioned by the limitations of our senses, and there is some other reality much larger and more complex than we are able to perceive. The effect I get from Mac-Caig's metaphorical explosiveness, or from that of poets such as Seamus Heaney, Sylvia Plath, or Ted Hughes, is not of some mystical world, but of multiple dimensions within a single perception. They are not discovering the extraordinary within the ordinary. They are, for the briefest of instants, perceiving something of reality as it truly is.

❖ ❖ ❖

What is poetry's role when the world is burning? Encroaching environmental disaster and the relentless wars around the world have had, it seems, a paralyzing, sterilizing effect on much American poetry. It is less the magnitude of the crises than our apparent immunity to them, this death on which we all thrive, that is spinning our best energies into esoteric language games, or complacent retreats into nostalgias of form or subject matter, or shrill denunciations of a culture whose privileges we are not ready to renounce—or, more accurately, do not even know how to renounce. There is some fury of clarity, some galvanizing combination of hope and lament, that is much needed now, but it sometimes seems that we—and I use the plural seriously, I don't exempt myself—are anxiously waiting for the devastation to reach our very streets, as it one day will, it most certainly will.

❖ ❖ ❖

But the fight is quiet sometimes too. Even for those in hell. Bonhoeffer: "It will be the task of our generation, not to 'seek great things,' but to save and preserve our souls out of the chaos, and to realize that it is the only thing we can carry as a 'prize' from the burning building."

✦ ✦ ✦

What is the difference between a cry of pain that is also a cry of praise and a cry of pain that is pure despair? Faith? The cry of faith, even if it is a cry against God, moves toward God, has its meaning in God, as in the cries of Job. The cry of faithlessness is the cry of the damned, like Dante's souls locked in trees that must bleed to speak, their release from pain only further pain. How much of twentieth-century poetry, how much of my own poetry, is the cry of the damned? But this is oversimplified. It doesn't account for a poet like A. R. Ammons, who had no religious faith at all but whose work has some sort of undeniable lyric transcendence. Perhaps this: a cry that seems to at once contain and release some energy that is not merely the self, that does not end at despair but ramifies, however darkly, beyond it, is a metaphysical cry. And to make such a cry is, even in the absence of definitions, a definition, for it establishes us in relation to something that is beyond ourselves. Ammons:

> . . . if you can
> send no word silently healing, I
>
> mean if it is not proper or realistic
> to send word, actual lips saying
>
> these broken sounds, why, may we be
> allowed to suppose that we can work
>
> this stuff out the best we can and
> having felt out our sins to their

deepest definitions, may we walk with
you as along a line of trees, every

now and then your clarity and warmth
shattering across our shadowed way:

—FROM *GLARE*

✣ ✣ ✣

Can you build a vocabulary of faith out of a rhetoric first made of
dread and then stand behind this new language? Is faith created
by a shift in rhetoric, one that can be consciously constructed, or
must there be a shattering experience, one that trashes the old words
for things?

—FANNY HOWE

There must be a shattering experience. Words are tied ineluctably
to the world. Language has its bloodlines, through history and
through our own beating hearts. "To change your language," writes
Derek Walcott, "you must change your life," though that still smacks
of the will. Humans—especially artists—love to imagine that they
might will themselves into new dispositions of self and soul. Otherwise it's all waiting, all readiness for a change that may never come.

Does that mean that no artist ever changes from inside? That
one cannot build a vocabulary of faith out of what Fanny Howe
calls "a rhetoric of dread"? That the work, when it has become fed
by nothing but absence, emptiness, despair, is for nothing?

Yes. Sometimes the work is for nothing and should be stopped.
You work your way as far as you can in one direction and then life
either changes you or not. The mistake many young artists make is
in thinking they can will such changes, or—much more dangerous—
float close to the fires of circumstance and suffering without being
burned:

Oh, should a child be left unwarned
That any song in which he mourned
Would be as if he prophesied?
It were unworthy of the tongue
To let the half of life alone
And play the good without the ill.
And yet t'would seem that what is sung
In happy sadness by the young,
Fate has no choice but to fulfill.

—ROBERT FROST, "THE WIND
AND THE RAIN"

✢ ✢ ✢

I've always been struck—haunted, really—by Wallace Stevens's phrase, in his great poem "Sunday Morning," "Death is the mother of beauty." Like that Robert Bringhurst poem I quoted at the beginning of this chapter, Stevens's line was practically tattooed on my brain for years; it was a kind of credo by which I lived. Or, as "Poŝtolka" makes clear, almost lived. It's the old carpe diem cry, Gather ye rosebuds while ye may, etc. etc. Except that Stevens, unlike Horace and Herrick, isn't encouraging haste and excess in the face of time slipping from one's grasp. "Sunday Morning," right from its famous first lines, is all about slowness and deliberation, about savoring experience:

Complacencies of the peignoir, and late
Coffee and oranges in a sunny chair,
And the green freedom of a cockatoo
Upon a rug, mingle to dissipate
The holy hush of ancient sacrifice.

No, Stevens believed that a concentration on death concentrates life, that we cannot see life clearly except through the lens of death, but that once we have seen it with such clarity, we can savor it. This is what I believed, and how I tried to live—until one day I found myself looking through the *actual* lens of death.

The view, it turned out, was quite different. From the moment I learned I had cancer—on my thirty-ninth birthday, from a curt voice mail message—not only was the world not intensified, it was palpably attenuated. I can still feel how far away everything—the people walking on the street beyond the window, the books on the shelf, my wife smiling up at me in the moment before I told her—suddenly seemed. And long after the initial shock, I felt a maddening, muffled quality to the world around me—which, paradoxically, went hand in hand with the most acute, interior sensations of pain. It seemed as if the numbness was not mine, but the world's, as if some energy had drained out of things. At some point I realized that for all my literary talk of the piquancy and poignancy that mortality imparts to immediate experience, part of my enjoyment of life had always been an unconscious assumption of its continuity. Not necessarily a continuity of reality itself—the moment *does* pass, of course—but a continuity in memory at least, and a future that the act of memory implies (there must be somewhere from which to remember). Life is short, we say, in one way or another, but in truth, because we cannot imagine our own death until it is thrust upon us, we live in a land where only other people die.

"Death is the mother of beauty" is a phrase that could only have been written by a man for whom death was an abstraction, a vaguely pleasant abstraction at that. Remove futurity from experience and you leach meaning from it just as surely as if you cut out a man's past. "Memory is the basis of individual personality," Miguel de Unamuno writes, "just as tradition is the basis of the collective personality of a people. We live in memory and by memory, and our spiritual life is at bottom simply the effort of our memory to persist, to transform itself into hope, the effort of our past to transform itself into our future."

In other words, we need both the past and the future to make our actions and emotions and sensations mean anything in the present.

Strictly speaking, though, the past and the future do not exist. They are both, to a greater or lesser degree, creations of the imagination. Anyone who tells you that you can live only in time, then, is not quite speaking the truth, since if we do not live out of time imaginatively, we cannot live in it actually. And if we can live out of time in our daily lives—indeed, if apprehending and inhabiting our daily lives *demands* that we in some imaginative sense live out of time—then is it a stretch to imagine the fruition of existence as being altogether outside of time?

✧ ✧ ✧

FROM A WINDOW
Incurable and unbelieving
in any truth but the truth of grieving,

I saw a tree inside a tree
rise kaleidoscopically

as if the leaves had livelier ghosts.
I pressed my face as close

to the pane as I could get
to watch that fitful, fluent spirit

that seemed a single being undefined
or countless beings of one mind

haul its strange cohesion
beyond the limits of my vision

over the house heavenwards.
Of course I knew those leaves were birds.

Of course that old tree stood
exactly as it had and would

(but why should it seem fuller now?)
and though a man's mind might endow

even a tree with some excess
of life to which a man seems witness,

that life is not the life of men.
And that is where the joy came in.

❖ ❖ ❖

I wrote this poem a few months after getting my diagnosis. Nothing was planned or deliberate about it. I didn't have the realization that an experience of reality can open into an experience of divinity and then go write a poem to illustrate my feelings. No, it was quite the reverse: I wrote the poem one day out of anguish, emptiness, grief—and it exploded into joy. I sought refuge in the half-conscious play of language and was rescued by a weave of meaning I never meant to make. The poem taught me something, and one of the things it taught me was that if you do not "think" of God, in whatever way you find to do that, if God has no relation to your experience, if God is not *in* your experience, then experience is always an end in itself, and always, I think, a dead end. Not only does experience open into nothing else, but that ulterior awareness, that spirit-cleansing whiff of the ultimate, never comes into the concrete details of existence either. You can certainly enjoy life like this; you can have a hell of a time. But I would argue that life remains *merely* something to be enjoyed, and that not only its true nature but also something within your true nature remains inert, unavailable, mute.

✤ ✤ ✤

"From a Window" was one of a handful of poems I wrote after my diagnosis that gave me some sense of purchase and promise: the terrible vagueness of things was dispelled for a moment and I could see where I was standing, and could feel a way forward. (*Feel* a way forward: if someone had asked me at the time if I believed in an afterlife, I would have said no. Yet my poems kept conjuring their eccentric heavens, kept prodding me toward new ways of understanding that verb "believe.") It was puzzling, then, and troubling, to find myself as time went on writing poems that seemed to give up the gains I had made, seemed not simply devoid of divinity, but to relish that fact:

> It is good to sit even a rotting body
> in sunlight uncompromised
> by God, or lack of God,
>
> to see the bee beyond
> all the plundered flowers
> air-stagger toward you
>
> and like a delicate helicopter
> hover above your knee
> until it finds you to be
>
> not sweet but at least
> not flinching, its hair-legs
> on the hair of your leg

silvering
a coolness through you
like a soul of nerve.

Not only is there no God in this poem, the very possibility is pushed roughly to the side. And yet I felt some saving otherness everywhere in me and around me when I wrote it. There is no possibility of heaven in this poem; indeed there is an implicit contempt for the notion. And yet I felt—during that brief marriage of word and world that poetry is—projected into dimensions of existence I could never have imagined before writing the poem, or could *only* have imagined but never felt. Can there be such a thing as an anti-devotional devotional poem? Hopkins and Herbert both thought that God circumscribed imagination, that faith required drawing certain lines inside of their own minds that they dared not cross, or if they crossed (for they certainly did), then they whipped themselves for it afterward. I understand the dilemma but disagree with the solution. If faith requires you to foreclose on an inspiration, surely it is not faith.

✦ ✦ ✦

The question of exactly which art is seeking God, and seeking to be in the service of God, is more complicated than it might seem. There is something in all original art that will *not* be made subject to God, if we mean by being made "subject to God" a kind of voluntary censorship or willed refusal of the mind's spontaneous and sometimes disturbing intrusions into, and extensions of, reality. But that is not how that phrase ought to be understood. In fact we come closer to the truth of the artist's relation to divinity if we think not of being made subject to God, but of being *subjected* to God—our individual subjectivity being lost and rediscovered within the reality of God. Human imagination is not simply our means of reaching out to

God but God's means of manifesting himself to us. It follows that any notion of God that is static is—since it asserts singular knowledge of God and seeks to limit his being to that knowledge—blasphemous. "God's truth is life," as Patrick Kavanagh says, "even the grotesque shapes of its foulest fire." One part of that truth, for even the most devout among us, is the void of godlessness—and sometimes, mysteriously, the joy of that void.

✦ ✦ ✦

The same impulse that leads me to sing of God leads me to sing of godlessness.

> God would have us know that we must live as men who manage our lives without him . . . The God who lets us live in the world without the working hypothesis of God is the God before whom we stand continually. Before God and with God we live without God.
>
> —DIETRICH BONHOEFFER

> The gods are back, companions. Right now they have just entered this life; but the words that revoke them, whispered underneath the words that reveal them, have also appeared that we might suffer together.
>
> —RENÉ CHAR

Sometimes God calls a person to unbelief in order that faith may take new forms.

O THOU MASTERING LIGHT

What were all those hours and years of reading and thinking? What had they done for him? He no more knew all the books he'd taken in than the water knows its flotsam, yet like that water he was thick and sluggish with it. He longed to be free of all that he once longed for, and began to imagine that there might come such a scouring (from where? with what?) that he might be, not wiped clean of what he'd so imperfectly learned, but emergent and changed on the other side of it. Not a purge, a passage. Then all these disparate pieces might cohere in him, cohere *as* him. The great irony, of course, the truth that came as all truths came to him now—too near to escape, too faint to savor—is that it was art that instilled in him this ideal of unity and clarity in the first place.

✦ ✦ ✦

Intellectuals and artists concerned with faith tend to underestimate the radical, inviolable innocence it requires. We read and read, write long, elaborate essays and letters, engage in endlessly inflected philosophical debates. We talk of poetry as prayer, artistic discipline as a species of religious devotion, doubt as the purest form of faith. These ideas are not inherently false. Indeed, there may be a deep truth in them. But the truth is, you might say, on the other side of innocence—*permanently*. That is, you don't once pass through religious innocence into the truths of philosophy or theology or literature, any more than you pass through the wonder of childhood into

the wisdom of age. Innocence, for the believer, remains the only condition in which intellectual truths can occur, and wonder is the
precondition for all wisdom.

❖ ❖ ❖

To be innocent is to retain that space in your heart that once heard
a still, small voice saying not your name so much as your nature,
and the wherewithal to say again and forever your wordless but lucid, your untriumphant but absolute, yes. You must protect this space
so that it can protect you. You must carry it with you through whatever milieu in which you find yourself growing too comfortable: the
seductive assurance and instant contempt of secularism, the hive-
like certainties of churches, the mental mazes of theology, the pro-
fessional vale of soul making that a life in literature can become.
Something in you must remain in you, voiceless even as you voice
your deepest faith, doubt, fear, dreams . . .

❖ ❖ ❖

Spiritual innocence is not naïveté. Quite the opposite. Spiritual innocence is a state of mind—or, if you prefer, a state of heart—in
which the life of God, and a life in God, are not simply viable but
the sine qua non of all knowledge and experience, not simply durable but everlasting. Consider these lines from Patrick Kavanagh,
who has returned, in imagination or in fact, to the land of his
childhood:

I do not know what age I am,
I am no mortal age;
I know nothing of women,
Nothing of cities,

I cannot die
Unless I walk outside these whitethorn hedges.
                    —FROM "INNOCENCE"

The poignancy of these lines inheres precisely in the fact that in the world outside of the poem, the poet is acutely aware of his age, has experience of women and cities, and knows that he will most definitely die—all because he did one day walk outside the "whitethorn hedges" of childhood. But the poem is not some facile, nostalgic assertion in defiance of this knowledge. It implies the annihilating powers of age, death, romantic failure, industrial destruction, and admits, within the context of linear time, its inadequacy as a bulwark against these things. At the same moment, though, it asserts the powers of youth, life, love, memory—powers that, paradoxically, exist only if they have been lost. To experience these lines fully is to feel at once a deep lament from outside of the poem and an utter exultation from within it, and *no necessary contradiction between these two truths*. Any man who would save his life must lose it, as Christ said.

✦ ✦ ✦

After I was diagnosed with cancer seven years ago, my wife and I found ourselves—and that's just what it felt like, that suggestion of passivity and chance—walking through the doors of the little church at the end of our block. I'd passed right by the church every day for three years on my way to the train and work downtown, but I couldn't even have told you what denomination it was. I wasn't tuned in to churches. Or to Christianity.

I was, however, tuned in to *something*. When I look back at some of the things I wrote in my twenties and thirties, I am struck by a strong sense of negative energy. Not negative as in sorrowful or depressive (though there's some of that), but negative in the contemporary scientific sense of something missing or indefinable, some strong charge whose source is unknown. "A loss of something ever felt I," writes Emily Dickinson, the votary and victim of this energy par excellence:

> The first that I could recollect
> Bereft I was—of what I knew not
> Too young that any should suspect
>
> A Mourner walked among the children
> I notwithstanding went about
> As one bemoaning a Dominion
> Itself the only Prince cast out—
>
> Elder, Today, a session wiser
> And fainter, too, as Wiseness is—
> I find myself still softly searching
> For my Delinquent Palaces—

There were several things that began to transform this energy, to give it form in my life rather than simply on the page. (No doubt it had "form" in my life previously, but its form was in effect the absence of form, a studied hovering just this side of any belief or commitment coherent enough to be at risk.) I stopped writing for a long time—several years—and without poetry to release the pressure of that mysterious, animate absence, it began to devour me. I don't want to overdramatize things. I know what "suicide ideation" is, and know how impotent that phrase is in the face of the actual terror it tries to name. That's not what was happening. It was more that the world went gray for me, and I couldn't accomplish even the simplest actions without great difficulty, the very air viscous and inhibiting. I thought often, and intimately, of the first stanza of Philip Larkin's devastating poem "Aubade":

I work all day, and get half-drunk at night.
Waking at four to soundless dark, I stare.
In time the curtain-edges will grow light.
Till then I see what's really always there:
Unresting death, a whole day nearer now,
Making all thought impossible but how
And where and when I shall myself die.

And that is the issue, isn't it? Death? That crashing cataract that comes to us, from this distance, as the white noise of life, that ur-despair that underlies all the little prickly irritations and anxieties that alcohol is engineered to erase.

Then I fell in love. It was that sudden, the rift in my life and mind that stark. Perhaps I'd never met the right person, as they say, and at thirty-seven years old finally got lucky. Perhaps the interior clarity and candor that one needs for real love had, in my case, always been clouded by the need to create, life deflected by art, and the enforced silence freed me to feel in more immediate ways. Whatever the case, when I met Danielle, not only was that gray veil between me and the world ripped aside, colors aching back into things, but all the particulars of the world suddenly seemed in excess of themselves, and thus more truly themselves. We, too, were part of this enlargement: it was as if our love demanded some expression beyond the blissful intensity our two lives made. I thought for years that any love had to be limiting, that it was a zero-sum game: what you gave with one part of yourself had to be taken from another. In fact, the great paradox of love, and not just romantic love, is that a closer focus may go hand in hand with a broadened scope. "To turn from everything to one face," writes Elizabeth Bowen, "is to find oneself face to face with everything."

And that's exactly what happened. Turning inward turned me outward too, to a world made radiant by my ability to believe in it. I have already mentioned the prayers that, long before the diagnosis, we began saying before our evening meals. How awkward and self-conscious we were at first, searching for some form in which to put, mostly, our praise, some sense of a being—or Being itself—to receive it. I think often of these early, furtive, innocent efforts at prayer. The beacon and bulwark they were when the devastation came.

❖ ❖ ❖

And this: that church at the end of our block turned out to be part of the United Church of Christ. The sanctuary was small, starkly beautiful, less than half filled with a mix of old German immigrants, a smattering of hipsters and upscale parents, and a couple of people who seemed homeless or headed there. The preacher had real presence. Tall, striking, clearly literary, he was definitely not the sort of person you expect to be leading a struggling little urban church. The service, too, was a surprise. After welcoming gays and lesbians, the preacher spoke inspiringly of the church as a place where our individual and communal needs and instincts were reconciled. His sermon was as witty and entertaining as it was theologically sophisticated and discomfiting. Its essence was how the void of God and the love of God come together in the mystery of the cross. I didn't really understand that notion then, but I felt, as did Danielle, oddly lightened by contemplating it. We filled out a visitors card but, hedging our bets, slipped out the side door to avoid having to meet the preacher.

But the next morning, he e-mailed me. We had an interesting exchange about churches, backgrounds, poetry. I revealed that I had "health problems" but nothing further. He said he hoped to see us again, if not in church then at least in the neighborhood, since he and his family lived in the parsonage and thus just a few houses down from us. And that was it.

Meanwhile my days were manic and scattered, my nights wakeful and anguished. We traveled to Boston to see a specialist, at the time the only person in North America who was doing research on my particular disease, and he terrified us by speculating— irresponsibly, it now seems to me—that my symptoms suggested that the cancer might already have caused amyloidosis in my heart: a death sentence.

That was the cloud I was walking under early one bright winter morning, maybe a week after the exchange of e-mails with the preacher, when I heard my name. I turned around to see him half running down the street toward me as he tried to pull a flannel shirt on over his T-shirt, careful not to trip over his untied shoes. I was in no mood to chat, especially not to an enthusiastic preacher, and all my thoughts were hostile. But I stopped, we had a kind of introduction as he tied his shoes, and then he asked if he could walk me to the train station. Those days are a blur to me, but I remember two things from that morning very clearly. I remember Matt straining to find some language that would be true to his own faith and calling and at the same time adequate to the tragedy and faithlessness—the tragedy *of* faithlessness—that he perceived in me. And I remember when we parted there was an awkward moment when the severity of my situation and our unfamiliarity with each other left us with no words, and in a gesture that I'm sure was completely unconscious, he placed his hand over his heart for just a second as a flicker of empathetic anguish crossed his face. It sliced right through me. It cut through the cloud I was living in and let the plain day pour its balm upon me. It was, I am sure, one of those moments when we enact and reflect a mercy and mystery that are greater than we are, when the void of God and the love of God, incomprehensible pain and the peace that passeth understanding, come together in a simple human act. We stood for a minute in the aftermath, not talking, and then went our suddenly less separate ways.

✥ ✥ ✥

When I was young, there was a notion among the believers I knew—and I didn't know anyone who *wasn't* a believer—that to feel the presence of God required that one seek God constantly, that one's spiritual instincts demanded the same sort of regular exercise as the muscles of one's body. The great fear was not that God would withdraw, but that one's capacity to perceive him would atrophy. I think of this when I hear people say that they have no religious impulse whatsoever, or when I hear believers, or would-be believers, express a sadness and frustration that they have never been absolutely overpowered by God. I always want to respond: Really? You have never felt overwhelmed by, and in some way inadequate to, an experience in your life, have never felt something in yourself staking a claim beyond your self, some wordless mystery straining through words to reach you? *Never?* Religion is not made of these moments; religion is the means of making these moments part of your life rather than merely radical intrusions so foreign and perhaps even fearsome that you can't even acknowledge their existence afterward. Religion is what you *do* with these moments of over-mastery in your life, these rare times in which you are utterly innocent. It is a means of preserving and honoring something that, ultimately, transcends the elements of whatever specific religion you practice.

✧ ✧ ✧

O hunger
Where all have mouths of desire and none
Is willing to be eaten: I am so glad
To come accidentally upon
My self at the end of a tortuous road
And have learned with surprise that God
Unworshipped withers to the Futile One.

—PATRICK KAVANAGH, FROM "AUDITORS IN"

✧ ✧ ✧

The frustration we feel when trying to explain or justify God, whether to ourselves or to others, is a symptom of knowledge untethered from innocence, of words in which no silence lives, of belief occurring wholly on a human plane. Innocence returns us to the first call of God, to any moment in our lives when we were rendered mute with awe, fear, wonder. Absent this, there is no sense in arguing for God in order to convince others, for we ourselves are not convinced.

✧ ✧ ✧

The spiritual efficacy of all encounters is determined by the amount of personal ego that is in play. If two people meet and disagree fiercely about theological matters but agree, silently or otherwise, that God's love creates and sustains human love, and that whatever else may be said of God is subsidiary to this truth, then even out of what seems great friction there may emerge a peace that—though it may not end the dispute, though neither party may be "convinced" of the other's position—nevertheless enters and nourishes one's notion of, and relationship with, God. Without this radical openness, all arguments about God are not simply pointless but pernicious, for each person is in thrall to some lesser conception of ultimate truth and asserts not love but a lesson, not God but himself.

✧ ✧ ✧

I have read so much theology in the past few years, yet in conversations with other Christians I am consistently made conscious of being in some way balked when trying to describe my notions of the nature of God, the meaning of the cross, Christianity's place with regard to other religions, etc. It isn't that these conversations aren't productive, but inevitably their benefit, for me at least, inheres wholly in the contact with another person of faith rather than in any new foundation of knowledge. I am less frustrated with this state of affairs than I once was, so maybe I have learned *something* from all those years of forcing myself to formulate my positions on poetry, from convincing myself that I *knew my own mind*. And perhaps the relation of theology to belief is roughly the same as that between the mastery of craft and the making of original art: one must at the same time utterly possess and utterly forget one's knowledge in order to go beyond it.

✤ ✤ ✤

To say that one must live in uncertainty doesn't begin to get at the tenuous, precarious nature of faith. The minute you begin to speak with certitude about God, he is gone. We praise people for having strong faith, but strength is only one part of that physical metaphor: one also needs *flexibility*.

✤ ✤ ✤

I tell myself that I have no problem believing in God, if "belief" can be defined as some utter interior assent to a life that is both beyond and within this one, and if "assent" can be understood as at once active and unconscious, and if "God" is in some mysterious way both this action and its object, and if after all these qualifications this sentence still makes any effing sense. Clearly, I do have something of a "problem." Poetry, fiction, meditative or mystical writers along the lines of Thomas Merton, Meister Eckhart, Simone Weil—these things tease me toward faith, make me feel the claim on my being that is much stronger than the "I" that needs *belief*, the "I" for whom faith is doctrine rather than identity ("You are in me deeper than I am in me," as Augustine puts it). Hard-core theology, on the other hand, tends to leave me cold, even when—perhaps *especially* when—it convinces me. I honestly don't know whether I am describing something essential about the way we know God or merely my own weakness of mind.

✤ ✤ ✤

Truly being here is glorious. Even *you* knew it,
you girls who seemed to be lost, to go under—, in the filthiest
streets of the city, festering there, or wide open
for garbage. For each of you had an hour, or perhaps
not even an hour, a barely measureable time
between two moments—, when you were granted a sense
of being. Everything. Your veins flowed with being.
But we can so easily forget what our laughing neighbor
neither confirms nor envies. We want to display it,
to make it visible, though even the most visible happiness
can't reveal itself to us until we transform it, within.
> —RAINER MARIA RILKE, THE SEVENTH DUINO ELEGY,
> TRANSLATED BY STEPHEN MITCHELL

All right: But what does it mean to transform these moments of intense inward understanding of the world and experience? I think it can only mean that we carry them with us back into the welter of our lives, that we return to them not as refugees from experience, but as devotees of it, that we come to understand our moments (or moment, maybe there was only one, will ever be only one) of clear-spirited existence in terms of all the life that is so obviously not, and vice versa.

The art critic Edgar Wind once accused Rilke of having "an emotionally untainted sense of form," meaning that he made these perfect artifacts that seemed to be about experiences he had never completely had. The very perfection of the form depended upon the detachment of the artist, but according to Wind, you could always feel that detachment within the perfection. The form wasn't compromised—it was perfect—but the feeling was.

Well, it is certainly possible to have an emotionally untainted (i.e., solitary) sense of spiritual experience, even to come to value spiritual experience precisely for this fact: it removes you from the chaos of ordinary consciousness, from the needs and demands of other people, from the dirty business of human love. But there is a death in this. Solitude is an integral part of any vital spiritual life, but spiritual experience that is *solely* solitary inevitably leads to despair.

But I don't want to lose Rilke's main point in the Seventh Duino Elegy, which is that spiritual experiences must be transformed within us, that there is hard work of inwardness to do, of consciousness, before those experiences become available to the rest of our lives. And I don't want to suggest that he himself failed at this. First of all, we can judge no one other than ourselves in this regard, and second, late in his life Rilke wrote this, in a letter to Ilse Jake:

The comprehensible slips away, is transformed; instead of possession one learns relationship, and there arises a namelessness that must begin once more in our relations with God if we are to be complete and without evasion. The experience of feeling him recedes behind an infinite delight in everything that can be felt; all attributes are taken away from God, who is no longer sayable, and fall back into creation, into love and death.

✤ ✤ ✤

I am struck by this: "But we can so easily forget what our laughing neighbor / neither confirms nor envies." What about these "laughing neighbors"? Surely we have all had the experience of having an intensely inward perception deflated within us by some non-reaction of the world, by pure indifference. (Disputatious rage or a kind of clock-minded logic—e.g., the "New Atheists"—is easier to take. Equally useless in terms of understanding and preserving your experience, but easier to ignore and move away from.) But the other, the laughing neighbor, this wounds us, and it does so because every genuine impulse of inwardness contains a little propulsion back toward the world and other people. In fact, as I've said, this is how you ascertain the truth of spiritual experience: it propels you back toward the world and other people, and not simply more deeply within yourself. This blankness to faith, this indifference that doesn't even reach the level of resistance, it is simply one of those weakening influences that we must push through. And without ego, without thinking ourselves superior, for we don't know all the ways in which God manifests himself or why some people in our lives, even some whom we most love, seem immune to inwardness. Perhaps we are the weak ones, and God comes to us inwardly only because we have failed to perceive him in the crying child, in the nail driven cleanly into the wood, in the ordinary dawn sun that merely to see clearly is sufficient prayer and praise.

✤ ✤ ✤

There is no clean intellectual coherence, no abstract ultimate meaning to be found, and if this is not recognized, then the compulsion to find such certainty becomes its own punishment. This realization is not the end of theology, but the beginning of it: trust no theory, no religious history or creed, in which the author's personal faith is not actively at risk.

✤ ✤ ✤

You know the value of your doubt by the quality of the disquiet that it produces in you. Is it a furious, centrifugal sort of anxiety that feeds on itself and never seems to move you in any one direction? Is it an ironclad compulsion to refute, to find in even the most transfiguring experiences, your own or others', some rational or "psychological" explanation? Is it an almost religious commitment to doubt itself, an assuredness that absolute doubt is the highest form of faith? There is something static and self-enthralled about all these attitudes. Honest doubt, what I would call devotional doubt, is marked, it seems to me, by three qualities: humility, which makes one's attitude impossible to celebrate; insufficiency, which makes it impossible to rest; and mystery, which continues to tug you upward—or at least outward—even in your lowest moments. Such doubt is painful—more painful, in fact, than any of the other forms—but its pain is active rather than passive, purifying rather than stultifying. Far beneath it, no matter how severe its drought, how thoroughly your skepticism seems to have salted the ground of your soul, faith, durable faith, is steadily taking root.

✤ ✤ ✤

The Gospels vary quite a bit in their accounts of Jesus' resurrection and the ensuing encounters he had with people, but they are quite consistent about one thing: many of his followers doubted him, sometimes even when he was staring them in the face. This ought to be heartening for those of us who seek belief. If the disciples of Christ could doubt not only firsthand accounts of his resurrection but the very fact of his face in front of them, then clearly, doubt has little to do with distance from events. It is in some way the seed of Christianity itself, planted in the very heart of him (*My God, my God, why hast thou forsaken me?*) who is at once our God and our best selves, and it must be torn terribly, wondrously open in order to flower into living faith.

But how does that happen? Here, too, the Gospel stories are helpful. Just as some of Jesus' first-century followers could not credit the presence of the risen Christ, so our own blindness, habit, and fear form a kind of constant fog that keeps us from seeing, and thereby believing in, the forms that grace takes in our everyday lives. We may think that it would be a great deal easier to believe if the world erupted around us, if some savior came down and offered as evidence the bloody scars in his side, but what the Gospels suggest is that this is not only wishful thinking but willful blindness, for in fact the world *is* erupting around us, Christ *is* very often offering us the scars in his side. What we call doubt is often simply dullness of mind and spirit, not the absence of faith at all, but faith latent in the lives we are not quite living, God dormant in the world to which we are not quite giving our best selves.

❖ ❖ ❖

Yes, but . . . the waking and the sleeping, the sludge of e-mails and appointments, the low-temperature life that is, for the most part, life: even if there are moments of intensity that seem to release us from this, surely any spiritual maturity demands an acknowledgment that there is not going to be some miraculous, transfiguring intrusion into reality. The sky will not darken and the dead will not speak; no voice from heaven is going to boom you back to a pre-reflective faith, nor will you feel, unless in death, a purifying fire that scalds all of consciousness like fog from the raw face of God. Is faith, then—assuming it isn't merely a form of resignation or denial— some sort of reconciliation with the implacable fact of matter, or is it a deep, ultimate resistance to it? Both. Neither. To have faith is to acknowledge the absolute materiality of existence while acknowledging at the same time the compulsion toward transfiguring order that seems not outside of things but within them, and within you—not an idea imposed upon the world, but a vital, answering instinct. Heading home from work, irritated by my busyness and the sense of wasted days, shouldering through the strangers who merge and flow together on Michigan Avenue, merge and flow in the mirrored facades, I flash past the rapt eyes and undecayed face of my grandmother, lit and lost at once. In a board meeting, bored to oblivion, I hear a pen scrape like a fingernail on a cell wall, watch the glasses sweat as if even water wanted out, when suddenly, at the center of the long table, light makes of a bell-shaped pitcher a bell that rings in no place on this earth. Moments, only, and I am aware even within them, and thus am outside of them, yet something in the very act of such attention has troubled the tyranny of the ordinary, as if the world at which I gazed, gazed at me, as if the lost face and the living crowd, the soundless bell and the mind in which it rings, all hankered toward—expressed some undeniable hope for—one end.

✦ ✦ ✦

And now I doubt the premise with which I began: that art is the source of my instinct toward unity rather than—like the theology I read, like scripture, like these all-too-inadequate fragments—a means of preserving and honoring that instinct. I distrust those skeptics who admit no spiritual element into their most transfiguring experiences because I am so easily and so often one of them, stepping outside of my own miraculous moments to inspect, analyze, explain.

> Having confessed, he feels
> That he should go down on his knees and pray
> For forgiveness for his pride, for having
> Dared to view his soul from the outside.
> —FROM "HAVING CONFESSED"

Kavanagh again. And that is the real issue, that the link not be broken, that every intellectual growth remain rooted in that early

experience of ultimate insight, ultimate unknowingness, every word
about God both responsive and responsible to the silence that is its
source. For all but the holy fools among us, rational thought—or
viewing the soul "from the outside"—is inevitable, whether through
theology, philosophy, science, or simply the narratives by means of
which we describe and understand our lives. But what sort of understanding could be emptier than one that diminishes or erases the
moments that made understanding essential in the first place? What
discipline more dubious than learning to see every logical flaw in
the light that once mastered you?

✥ ✥ ✥

O unworn world enrapture me, encapture me
In a web of fabulous grass and eternal voices by a beech.
Feed the gaping need of my senses. Give me ad lib
To pray unselfconsciously with overflowing speech
For this soul needs to be honored with a new dress woven
From green and blue things and arguments that cannot be
    proven.
　　　—PATRICK KAVANAGH, FROM "CANAL BANK WALK"

DEAR OBLIVION

I have never felt comfortable praying. I almost feel I should put the word in quotes, as I'm never quite sure that what I do deserves the name. I have a little litany of stations through which I move—thank you, help me, be with, forgive—but mostly I simply (simply!) try to subject myself to the possibility of God. I address God *as if.*

"We must believe in the real God in every way," says Simone Weil, "except that he does not exist, for we have not reached the point where he might exist." I don't take this to mean that if we achieve some state worthy of God, he will pop into being like a genie. Rather, I think Weil is suggesting that devotion to God, for modern believers, involves learning to inhabit—rather than simply trumping with dogma or literal scripture—those elements of our existence that seem inimical to his: limitedness, contingency, suffering, death.

Contemporary people whose lives are marked by a searching, scorching spiritual focus—whether it's conflicted believers, God-haunted agnostics, or even the neo-atheists whose very avidity gives them away—tend to be obsessed by *whether* God exists. What Weil is saying is that this is not beside the point exactly, but a misdirection: God exists apart from our notions of what it means to exist, and there is a sense in which our most pressing existential question has to be outgrown before it can be answered.

Religion has always emerged at the edge of what humans know. As that edge has been pushed further and further into the unknown, as our reach has extended into space and the atom and even the chemistry of our own needs and desires, some people have assumed that existence is, in the end, knowable. This not only contravenes centuries of human experience, duplicating the hubris that has doomed us so many times in the past, but more crucially, it violates, even desecrates, the most intimate, ultimate experiences of our own lives.

There are moments in every life when one is overwhelmed—in a "positive" sense, though there may very well be suffering—by reality; or, more accurately, overwhelmed by reality spilling its boundaries. It can happen when you fall in love or, after the early nullifying horror abates a bit, when the world returns sharper and starker after a dire diagnosis. It can happen when eternity, in the form of your first child, comes crying bloody and impossibly beloved into time. It can even happen—though much less dramatically and obviously, at least for me, at least so far—in prayer. At such moments it is not only as if we were suddenly perceiving something in reality we had not perceived before, but as if we ourselves were being perceived. It is as if the interstellar spaces, and all the random atoms into which we will one day vanish, turned a kind of incomprehensible but utterly comprehending attention toward us. It is as if oblivion whispered in our ears.

This is one aspect of God's nature, the infinite inhering in the specific, atomic (in every sense of that word) insights that disclose our beings and situate us in something larger than ourselves, even as they cast us back into brute reality—the daily responsibilities of caring for a child or the modulations of marriage, the terror and tedium of ongoing illness, or simply the hollow sound of your own voice attempting to pray. I suppose it is possible to knit a kind of spiritual life together out of these moments, for they do restore one's links to and with the earth; they do propel one forward into time and connections. For me, though, there is something too inchoate and sporadic to such a spiritual life: a devotion that hinges only on these rare intensities begins to seem, for me, like a discipline of memory.

An essential discipline, yes, but one that makes Being seem mostly in abeyance and life a long wait for God, who is knowable only in emotional extremity, and only then by a sort of tender oblivion.

Back to Weil. If part of what she encourages is implicit and passive, a letting go of our mind's most developed capacities in order to realize our mind's further capacities, another part—indeed the *first* part—is explicit and all action: "We must believe in the real God in every way." There are many ways to interpret this, of course, and religious factions will be fighting to the end of days over who exactly the "real God" is. For Weil, though, one thing is clear: to believe in God is a practical matter, faith a physical act renewed (or not) at every moment. For a Christian—which I think Weil was, although poignantly (tellingly?) she could never quite bring herself to be baptized and formally enter the church—this means believing in a God who is not apart from matter (or not merely that) but part of it, a God who does not simply enjoin us to participate fully in life, and specifically in the relationships within our lives, but a God who inheres *wholly* within those relationships.

For that is another aspect of God's nature, which is human nature, embodied in, and suffered through, Christ.

—for Christ plays in ten thousand places,
Lovely in limbs, and lovely in eyes not his,
To the Father through the features of men's faces.
—GERARD MANLEY HOPKINS

For all the intensity of our meditative moments, for all the necessity of "mystical" experiences that can never quite be translated into the terms of ordinary life, until our faith is rooted in and inextricable from our daily reality, those moments and experiences are as likely to wreck as to rescue us, because we cannot live up to them: they indict the mildness with which we drift through our days. The greatest mystery of those moments in our lives is that, in a way, there is no mystery: that is to say, the immense, ungraspable, mystical reality that overwhelms us is also the concrete, suffering, sometimes all-too-touchable face right in front of our eyes.

One day when I had gone to a little chapel near my office at lunchtime and was once more praying while wondering how and why and to whom I prayed, a man came in and eased into the pew directly across the aisle from me. As we were the only two people there, his choice of where to sit seemed odd, and irritating. Within a couple of minutes, all thought of God was gone into the man's constant movements and his elaborate sighs, and when I finally rose in exasperation, he stood immediately to face me. He had the sandblasted look of long poverty, the skeletal clarity of long addiction, and that vaguely aggressive abasement that truly tests the nature of one's charity. Very cunning, I noted, failing the test even as I opened my wallet: to stake out this little chapel, to prey upon the praying! For days then it nagged at me—not him, but it, the situation—which, I finally realized, was precisely the problem: how easily a fatal complacency seeps into even those acts we undertake as disciplines, and how comfortable we become with our own intellectual and spiritual discomfort. *Wondering how and why and to whom I prayed?* I felt almost as if God had been telling me, as if *Christ* were telling me (in church no less): get off your mystified ass and *do* something.

HIVE OF NERVES

It is time that the stone grew accustomed to blooming,
That unrest formed a heart.

—PAUL CELAN

At a dinner with friends the talk turns, as it often does these days, to the problem of anxiety: how it is consuming everyone; how the very technologies we have developed to save time and thereby lessen anxiety have only degraded the quality of the former and exacerbated the latter; how we all need to "give ourselves a break" before we implode. Everyone has some means of relief—tennis, yoga, a massage every Thursday—but the very way in which those activities are framed as apart from regular life suggests the extent to which that relief is temporary (if even that: a couple of us admit that our "recreational" activities partake of the same simmering, near-obsessive panic as the rest of our lives). There is something circular and static to our conversation, which doesn't end so much as fizzle indeterminately out, and though there is always some comfort in comparing maladies, I am left with the uneasy feeling that my own private anxieties have actually increased by becoming momentarily collective—or no, not that, increased by *not* becoming collective, increased by the reinforcement of my loneliness within a collective context, like that penetrating but enervating stab of self one feels sometimes in an anonymous crowd. It is a full day later before it occurs to me that not once, not in any form, not even with the ghost of a suggestion, did any of us mention God.

✤ ✤ ✤

The greatness of *Ulysses* is partly in the way it reveals the interior chaos of a single mind during a single day, and partly in the way it makes that idiosyncratic clamor universal. However different the textures of our own lives may be, Bloom's mind is our mind; the welter of impressions he suffers and savors is a storm we all know. And that is the book's horror, too: some form of this same fury of trivia is going on in the mind of every sentient person on the planet. How much cruelty is occasioned simply because of the *noise* that is within us: the din is too great to realize exactly what we are doing to others, or what is being done to others in our name. Thus an offhand remark, which leaves us as easily as a breath and which we think no more of than a breath, cuts a friend to the quick. And thus a whole country can be organized toward some collective insanity because there is no space in individuals to *think*.

✤ ✤ ✤

Something is off. Life passes and we do not recognize it. The past streams through us like molecules we can't perceive, and we miss the God who misses—as in longs for—us:

> I love the calm and custom of quick fingers weaving,
> The shuttle's buzz and hum, the spindle's bees.
> And look—arriving or leaving, spun from down,
> Some barefoot Delia barely touching the ground . . .
> What rot has reached the very root of us
> That we should have no language for our praise?

> What is, was; what was, will be again; and our whole lives'
> Sweetness lies in these meetings that we recognize.
>
> —OSIP MANDELSTAM, FROM "TRISTIA"

These meetings that we recognize—of them faith is made and sustained. They are not so much remembered as resurrected in us, little stitches of ordinary time that suddenly—a prick in the existential skin, a little dot of Being's blood—aren't. Is it merely certain temperaments—inclined to solitude and absence, feasting on distances—that are at once susceptible to these little epiphanies and yet slow to recognize them for what they are? Or is it a symptom of the times—distracted, busy, forward-rushing—that we are in? Or a symptom of time itself as we have come to understand it:

> We have constructed an environment in which we live a uniform,
> univocal secular time, which we try to measure and control in or-
> der to get things done. This "time frame" deserves, perhaps more
> than any other facet of modernity, Weber's famous description of
> a "stahlhartes Gehäuse" (iron cage).
>
> —CHARLES TAYLOR, *A SECULAR AGE*

✤ ✤ ✤

How does one remember God, reach for God, realize God in the midst of one's life if one is constantly being overwhelmed by that life? It is one thing to encourage contemplation, prayer, quiet spaces in which God, or at least a galvanizing consciousness of his absence ("Be present with your Want of a Deity, and you shall be present with the Deity," as the seventeenth-century poet Thomas Traherne put it), can enter the mind and heart. But the reality of contemporary American life—which often seems like a kind of collective ADHD—is that this consciousness requires a great deal of resistance, and how does one relax and resist at the same time?

✦ ✦ ✦

COMMUTE (1)
     O the screech and heat and hate
     we have for each day's commute,

     the long wait at the last stop
     before we go screaming

     underground, while the pigeons
     court and shit and rut

     insolently on the tracks
     because this train is always late,

     always aimed at only us,
     who when it comes with its

     blunt snout, its thousand mouths,
     cram and curse and contort

     into one creature, all claws and eyes,
     tunneling, tunneling, tunneling

     toward money.

✦ ✦ ✦

In the Gospels, Jesus is always talking to the crowds in parables, which he later explains to his disciples. The dynamic is odd in a couple of ways: either the parables are obvious and the explanations seem almost patronizing, or they are opaque and the explanations only compound their opacity. (Or could it be—and I confess to relishing this possibility—that the explanations illustrate Christ's wry sense of humor, which is nowhere else evident?) In any case, the notable point is just how little the explanations amount to, how completely the ultimate truths of the parables—just like dreams and poems—remain within their own occurrence.

Behind every urge to interpret is unease, anxiety. This can be a productive and necessary endeavor, whether it's literary criticism or theology or even the entire dogmas and rituals of a religion (since all religion is, ultimately, an attempt to interpret God and numinous experience). Such effort deepens and complicates our initial response, even as it gives us an aperture through which to see our moments of mystery, crisis, and revelation more clearly—to give them "meanings," to integrate them into our lives. The trouble comes when the effort to name and know an experience replaces the experience itself. Just as we seem to have grasped every level of meaning in a poem, the private and silent power that compelled us in the first place drains right out of it. Just as we plant the flag of faith on the mountain of doctrine and dogma it has taken every ounce of our intellect to climb, our vision becomes a "view," which is already clouding over and is in any event cluttered with the trash of others who have fought their way to this exact same spot. Nowhere to go now but down.

"If that's what he means," says the student to the poetry teacher, "why doesn't he just say it?" "If God is real," says the parishioner to the preacher, "why doesn't he simply storm into our lives and convince us?" The questions are vastly different in scale and relative importance, but their answers are similar. A poem, if it's a real one, in some fundamental sense means no more and no less than the moment of its singular music and lightning insight; it is its own code to its own absolute and irreducible clarity. A god, if it's a living one, is not outside of reality but in it, of it, though in ways it takes patience and imagination to perceive. Thus the uses and necessities of metaphor, which can flash us past our plodding resistance and habits into strange new truths. Thus the very practical effects of music, myth, and image, which tease us not out of reality, but deeper and more completely into it.

Christ speaks in stories as a way of preparing his followers to stake their lives on a story, because existence is not a puzzle to be solved, but a narrative to be inherited and undergone and transformed person by person. He uses metaphors because something essential about the nature of reality—its mercurial solidity, its mathematical mystery and sacred plainness—is disclosed within them. He speaks the language of reality—speaks in terms of the physical world—because he is reality's culmination and key (one of them, at any rate), and because "this people's mind has become dull; they have stopped their ears and shut their eyes. Otherwise, their eyes might see, their ears hear, and their mind understand, and then they might turn to me, and I would heal them."

✣ ✣ ✣

Live long enough in secular culture, long enough to forget that it *is* secular culture, and at some point religious belief becomes preposterous to you. Atavistic. Laughable. I know this was true for me. Never mind that many of my favorite writers were quite obviously religious—Simone Weil, Marilynne Robinson, T. S. Eliot, George Herbert—or that I retained some intellectual respect for the "intellectual" side of Christianity—Meister Eckhart, Paul Tillich, Thomas Merton—still, the idea of giving my inchoate feelings of faith some actual content, never mind the thought of attending a church, this seemed not only absurd to me but an obvious weakness. To be a Christian was to flinch from contingency and death, both of which were the defining realities of contemporary life. To be a Christian was death for art, which depends on an attitude of openness and unknowingness (never mind the irony of an *imperative* of openness and unknowingness). It took a radical disruption of my life to allow me to see the sanity and vitality of this strange, ancient thing. There was no bolt-from-the-blue revelation or conversion or any of that. My old ideas simply were not adequate for the extremes of joy and grief that I experienced, but when I looked at my life through the lens of Christianity—or, more specifically, through the lens of Christ, as much of Christianity seemed (and still seems) *uselessly* absurd to me—it made sense. The world made sense. This distance between culture and Christ seems like a modern phenomenon, but I think it's probably always been the case. Even when Christianity is the default mode of a society, Christ is not. There is always some leap into what looks like absurdity, and there is always, for the one who makes that leap, some cost.

✤ ✤ ✤

I don't think the "answer" to the anxiety felt by everyone at that dinner party is Christianity. In fact I'm pretty sure that is not the case, as we represented several different traditions (including no tradition)—and anyway Christ is not an answer to existence, but a means of existing, and I am convinced that there is no permutation of man or mind in which he is not, in some form, present. This from the Catholic nun, Sara Grant, speaking about, and quoting from, the *Kena Upanishad:*

> Brahman is not "that which one knows," but that by which one knows, as though a crystal bowl were aware of the sun shining through it. "When he is known through all cognitions, he is rightly known."

But it seems to me you could quote Christ himself in support of this idea: "To believe in me is not to believe in me but in him who sent me; to see me is to see him who sent me."

I do think, though, that both the problem of, and the solution to, our individual anxiety is a metaphysical one. Some modern philosophers (Heidegger, Kierkegaard) have argued that existential anxiety proceeds from being unconscious of, or inadequately conscious of, death. True, I think, but I wonder if the emphasis might be placed differently, shifted from unconscious reaction to unrealized action: that is, our anxiety is less the mind shielding itself from death than the spirit's need to *be*. It is as if each of us were always hearing some strange, complicated music in the background of our lives, music that, so long as it remains in the background, is not simply distracting but manifestly unpleasant, because *it demands the attention we are giving to other things*. It is not hard to hear this music, but it is very difficult to learn to hear it *as* music.

✣ ✣ ✣

Who is it that clasps and kneads my naked feet, till they
   unfold,
till all is well, till all is utterly well? the lotus-lilies of the feet!

I tell you it is no woman, it is no man, for I am alone.
And I fall asleep with the gods, the gods
that are not, or that are
according to the soul's desire,
like a pool into which we plunge, or do not plunge.
                              —FROM "THERE ARE NO GODS"

The operative word in these lines from D. H. Lawrence, who wasn't a conventionally religious person, is "soul." It's a word that has become almost embarrassing for many contemporary people unless it is completely stripped of its religious meaning. Perhaps that's just what it needs sometimes: to be stripped of its "religious" meaning, in the sense that faith itself sometimes needs to be stripped of its social and historical encrustations and returned to its first, churchless incarnation in the human heart. That's what the twentieth century was, a kind of windstorm-scouring of all we thought was knowledge, and truth, and ours—until it became too strong for us, or we too weak for it, and "the self replaced the soul as the fist of survival" (Fanny Howe). Anxiety comes from the self as ultimate concern, from the fact that the self cannot bear this ultimate concern: it buckles and wavers under the strain, and eventually, inevitably, it breaks.

✣ ✣ ✣

"Glimmerings are what the soul's composed of," writes Seamus Heaney, an interesting—and, I think, accurate—thought, if the word "glimmerings" is read as both literal and metaphorical: the soul is not simply the agent that does the seeing (the entity to which metaphorical glimmerings are given), it is in some way the things that are seen (the world that glimmers); or, perhaps more accurately, the soul is the verb that makes an exchange between the self and reality—or the self and other selves—possible. It is the soul that turns perception into communication, and communication—even if it's just between one man and the storm of atoms around him—into communion.

✣ ✣ ✣

Faith steals upon you like dew: some days you wake and it is there. And like dew, it gets burned off in the rising sun of anxieties, ambitions, distractions.

✣ ✣ ✣

The meanings that God calls us to in our lives are never abstract. Though the call may ask us to redefine, or refine, what we know as life, it does not demand a renunciation of life in favor of something beyond it. Moreover, the call itself is always composed of life. That is, it is not some hitherto unknown voice to which we respond; it is life calling to life. People think that diagnosing the apostle Paul with epilepsy or some related disorder nullifies any notion that God might truly have revealed something of himself on that road to Damascus. But God speaks to us by speaking through us, and any meaning we arrive at in this life is composed of the irreducible details of the life that is around us at any moment. "I think there is no light in the world / but the world," writes George Oppen. "And I think there is light."

✤ ✤ ✤

There is a distinction to be made between the anxiety of daily existence, which we talk about endlessly, and the anxiety of existence, which we rarely mention at all. The former fritters us into dithering, distracted creatures. The latter attests to—and, if attended to, discloses—our souls. And yet it is a distinction without a difference, perhaps, and as crucial to eventually overcome as it is to initially understand. To be truly alive is to feel one's ultimate existence within one's daily existence. All those trivial, frittering anxieties acquire, even if only briefly, a lightness, a rightness, a meaning. So long as anxiety is merely something to be alleviated, it is not life, or we are not alive enough to experience it as such.

✤ ✤ ✤

I don't mean to be describing an intellectual transformation, or a transformation that is available only to "intellectuals." I suppose that for many people—people inclined to read a book like this one, for instance—the transformation might *seem* to begin with a mental decision and a definite application of the will. In fact, I think taking such a step indicates that some rift of meaning and feeling has already opened inside of us and we are clutching—consciously or unconsciously—at the rock face and rubble above this sudden abyss. In the end, if we are to integrate our anxieties into our spiritual lives and thereby alleviate those anxieties, any merely intellectual understanding of them is inadequate.

Consciousness among contemporary Western intellectuals is an "apprehensive" quality: that is to say, we become conscious by taking hold of, or apprehending, our selves and reality, by standing apart from them—and, not at all coincidentally (for where, exactly, are we standing?), we grow apprehensive as we do so. There are other, fuller ways of being in the world, which Eastern religions, as well as Christian mysticism, strive to articulate. (Meister Eckhart: "It is not that we should abandon, neglect, or deny our inner self, but we should learn to work precisely in it, with it, and from it in such a way that interiority turns into effective action and effective action leads back to interiority, and we become used to acting without any compulsion.") But again, the best evidence comes not from books, but from people, some of whom would never think to pick up a book. And suddenly I am seeing my grandmother again, recalling that habit of mind too attentive to be called passive, too intuitive to be called thought. I am thinking (*thinking!*) of a presence so in love with life, so in tune with time, that death seemed only to drive her further in:

> She who in her last days loved too well to lose
> A single weed to namelessness, in creosote,
> Blue grama, goatsbeard that is not thriving, is,
> Amid the cattails' brittle whisper whispers
> *O Law', Honey, ain't this a praiseful thing.*
> —FROM "THE RESERVOIR"

✤ ✤ ✤

The itch inside of contentment, or the itch that perhaps *is* contentment, as if despite our problems with anxiety, inner rest required
outer restlessness, as if peace with ourselves and our times were found
only *within* frenzy. Or, for some, never found at all. W. B. Yeats:

> Through winter-time we call on spring,
> And through the spring on summer call,
> And when abounding hedges ring
> Declare that winter's best of all;
> And after that there's nothing good
> Because the spring-time has not come—
> Nor know that what disturbs our blood
> Is but its longing for the tomb.
>   —"THE WHEEL"

This is life as pure death wish. There is a sense in which Yeats is
right: what we seek is meaning for our ceaseless, anxious, and always-
anticipatory actions, and death is part of that meaning. Any life that
does not take account of death, that does not, in one way or another,
hear the annihilating silence inside every sound, the nullifying stillness within every action, is a life that can neither harness nor re-
dress that dark energy—which is to say, a life of which death already
has possession. Yeats's mistake, though (in this one poem, I mean),
is to make death the *entire* meaning of life, which ultimately makes
not only our anxieties but also our actions meaningless.

Here's another take, by George Herbert:

> When God at first made man,
> Having a glass of blessings standing by;
> Let us (said he) pour on him all we can:
> Let the world's riches, which dispersèd lie,
>   Contract into a span.

So strength first made a way,
Then beauty flowed, then wisdom, honor, pleasure:
When almost all was out, God made a stay,
Perceiving that, alone of all his treasure,
    Rest in the bottom lay.

For if I should (said he)
Bestow this jewel also on my creature,
He would adore my gifts instead of me,
And rest in Nature, not the God of Nature:
    So both should losers be.

Yet let him keep the rest,
But keep them with repining restlessness:
Let him be rich and weary, that at least,
If goodness lead him not, yet weariness
    May toss him to my breast.

—"THE PULLEY"

In this poem our very restlessness is a gift, as it reminds us, even when we are most content, what we most need and why we are on this earth at all. The poem is perhaps theologically suspect (why this rat's maze of a world for a known result?) but intuitively true. We are driven ceaselessly onward in this life and are certain of our desires only until we realize them, at which point they seem to dissolve and shimmer farther off, like a heat mirage on a road down which we can't stop racing. Unlike Yeats, though, for whom that road ends at a massive wall into which we finally, fatally slam, for Herbert the very permanence of our longing is proof of longing's eventual fruition. That doesn't mean that this fruition is forever forestalled. It isn't "heaven," exactly, except insofar as we learn to see, as he says in another poem, "Heaven in ordinary."

✦ ✦ ✦

At first, attending to the anxiety of existence can seem like a zero-sum game. Any attention turned toward spiritual truth is attention turned away from all we have come to think of as "life." Thus we parcel out our moments of devotion—a church service here and there, a walk in the woods, a couple of hours of meditation a week—all the while maintaining the frenzy of our usual existence outside of those moments. This is inevitable, for the initial demands of any coherent spiritual life are intense, but it is not sustainable, for the soul is not piecemeal. We are left with this paradox: only by hearing the farthest call of consciousness can we hear the call of ordinary life, but only by claiming the most mundane and jangling details of our lives can that rare and ulterior music of the soul merge with what Seamus Heaney calls "the music of what happens."

✦ ✦ ✦

It is a strange thing how sometimes merely to talk honestly of God, even if it is only to articulate our feelings of separation and confusion, can bring peace to our spirits. You thought you were unhappy because this or that was off in your relationship, this or that was wrong in your job, but the reality is that your sadness stemmed from your aversion to, your stalwart avoidance of, God. The other problems may very well be true, and you will have to address them, but what you feel when releasing yourself to speak of the deepest needs of your spirit is the fact that no other needs could be spoken of outside of that context. You cannot work on the structure of your life if the ground of your being is unsure.

✦ ✦ ✦

The first step in the life of the spirit is learning to let yourself experience those moments when life and time seem at once suspended and concentrated, that paradox of attentive oblivion out of which any sustaining faith grows. These moments may not be—and at first almost certainly will not be—"meditative." They are more likely to break into your awareness, or into what you thought was awareness ("inbreaking" is the theological term for Christ's appearance in the world and in our lives—there is no coaxing it, no way to earn it, no way to prepare except to hone your capacity to respond, which is, finally, your capacity to experience life, and death). This is why we cannot separate one part of our existence, or one aspect of our awareness, from another, for there is a seed of peace in the most savage clamor. There is a kind of seeing that, fusing attention and submission, becomes a kind of being, wherein you may burrow into the very chaos that buries you, and even the most binding ties can become a means of release.

✣ ✣ ✣

COMMUTE (2)

There is a dreamer
all good conductors

know to look for
when the last stop is made

and the train is ticking cool,
some lover, loner, or fool

who has lived so hard
he jerks awake

in the graveyard,
where he sees

coming down the aisle
a beam of light

whose end he is,
and what he thinks are chains

becoming keys . . .

✦ ✦ ✦

Keys to what, though? For I can't end with that flourish of poetry
and privacy. Art, like religious devotion, either adds life or steals it.
It is never neutral. Either it impels one back toward life or is merely
one more means of keeping life at arm's length. (The subject matter
and tone of art have less to do with this than many people think:
nothing palls the soul like a forced epiphany, and one can be elated
and energized by a freshly articulate despair.) *Keys to what?* In this
poem, the keys are, on one level, to the constraints felt in the earlier
section (the miserable commute, the crush of others, the "screech and
heat and hate"), which prove to be their own means of release ("what
he thinks are chains / becoming keys"). On another level, the keys
are to the mysteries of death; or, rather, the key is to the blunt, immutable, physical fact of death (the train "graveyard"), which opens,
if only for a moment, to reveal a mystery.

And now it's over. Now the man on the train, like the man who
imagined him (me!), like Paul God-struck outside of Damascus (alas,
it wasn't quite like that for me), must move. Now the revelation either becomes part of his life or is altogether lost to it. Either his actions acquire a deeper purpose and begin to echo and counterpoint
each other, or the moment and the man slip back into unfeeling
frenzy, and the screech and heat and hate of his days lock metalli-
cally around him again.

Death is the only lens for true transcendence, but paradoxically, transcendence is possible only when we cease being conscious of our own deaths. I don't mean that we are *unconscious* of our own deaths, but that we pass through what we think of as consciousness—that "apprehensiveness" I mentioned, that standing-apart-from and taking-hold-of—into something more profound. What you feel in amateur photographs—it's a large part of the poignancy—is the pressure, or the lack of pressure, actually, of all the reality missing from the picture, which is really just a chopped-off piece of life. An artist, on the other hand, makes you feel just how much missing life is contained within a given image: it is as if the image is surrounded with, enlivened and even created by, the invisible, the unknowable, the absent. It's not accurate to say that someone who has learned to see like this has *forgotten* that there is a lens between himself and life. It's more that the lens has become so intuitive and fluent that it's just another, clearer eye.

That dinner party with which I began this chapter was a failure of mine—not of nerve, exactly, for nothing I have said here had even crossed my mind at that point. No, it was a failure of consciousness, which is always a spiritual failure. I believe there is a kind of existence in which meditation and communication, epiphanies and busyness, death and life, God and not—all these apparent antinomies are merged and made into one awareness. I am a long way from realizing such perception myself, but I have lifted the lens to my eyes—there is a sense in which it must be voluntarily lifted, even if, perhaps especially if, it has been roughly thrust there by circumstance—and am learning.

GOD IS NOT BEYOND

If you come to an idea of faith as "first of all an intellectual assent" (Thomas Merton); or if you think of it not as a state of mind at all but as "being seized by Being itself" (Paul Tillich); or if you think of faith as primarily "faithfulness to an event" (Abraham Joshua Heschel) in the past in which you or even all of humanity were, in effect, seized by Being; or if you construct some sort of "inductive faith" (Peter Berger) out of the moments of transcendence in your ordinary life; or if you feel that faith is wholly a matter of grace and thus outside of man's control altogether (Karl Barth); or if you feel, as I do, that every one of these definitions has some truth in it— then you are still left with this question: *Why?* Why should existence be arranged so that our alienation from God is a given and we must forever fight our way not simply toward what he is but toward the whole notion *that* he is? If you let go of the literal creation story as it comes down to us through Genesis, if you let go of the Garden of Eden, the intellectual apple, the whole history of man's separation from God tied to the tongue of a talking snake; if you let go of these things—and who but a child could hold on to them—then you are left, paradoxically, with a child's insistent question: *Why?*

❖ ❖ ❖

Our natures—and nature itself—are not corrupt (or not entirely so) but unfinished. "All Creation groaneth and travaileth in pain together," says Paul, which is exactly right. But also this: all creation, including every atom of our selves, groaneth and travaileth *toward* something—not toward some ideal existence from which "sin" has irretrievably separated us, and not toward some heaven that is simply this existence times eternity. No. Faith is not faith in some state beyond change. Faith is faith *in* change. That this welter of cells entails for us great sorrow and difficulty is true. That uppercase Life requires our lowercase ones is beyond question. But there is great joy in this ongoing apocalypse as well ("apocalypse," meaning to uncover, to reveal), joy in reality's abundance and prodigality, in its atomic detail and essential indestructibility, and in the deep, implicit peace whose surest promise of reality is the miraculous capacity we have—in a work of art, a gesture of love, or any of the other ways in which we acknowledge the God who *is* this ever-perfecting process—to imagine it.

✤ ✤ ✤

To *imagine* it—this peace, this unity, this life beyond the one we're in—not necessarily to "believe" in it. To have faith in the meaning and final fruition of this impulse in us, but not to anxiously attempt to fill out that faith with content.

I have heard a well-known conservative preacher proclaim with full confidence that, given the clear message of John 14:2 ("In my father's house are many mansions . . ."), it is evident that in heaven there will be resplendent mansions for every person on earth who was saved by Jesus Christ. It's easy to mock this kind of literalism, but the fear (of death, of oblivion) from which it emerges is sometimes apparent even in liberal theologies. I once heard another sermon by a Congregationalist preacher that brilliantly evoked this instinct for eternity that every time-bound life contains. But then she flinched, insisting on the survival of individual consciousness as we now know it. Heaven, she said, whatever it is, will restore to us the relationships that we have lost, will heal this whole dear world that we are always losing.

This presumes too much. Death is here to teach us something, or to make us fit for something. To project ourselves beyond it is to violate not only the terms of this life, which include a clear-eyed awareness of the end no eye can pierce, but also, I suspect, of the next. The liberal preacher I mention above was addressing a large, prosperous, and secularly oriented church, and she assumed, rightly, that they would be resistant to her notions of heaven, that it would sound preposterous to their modern scientific sensibilities. That's the whole point, she argued: the very fact of our resistance to heaven is part of the warrant of its authenticity, for it reminds us of—it shocks us back into the presence of—the radical strangeness of our God. This seems to me misguided. It is not that conventional ideas of an afterlife are too strange; it is that they are not strange enough. It's not that the God of orthodox (or neo-orthodox) eschatology seems incredible; it's that he seems weakened by our fear of dying. Refusing heaven can be a form of faith if it's done to give God his true and terrible scope.

�֍ ✤ ✤

My God, my God, why hast thou forsaken me? We are given nothing else after these words from Christ on the cross, though it is not hard to imagine others that must have gone through his head: *Is it because I have not lived up to you, am not worthy of you? Is it because you are ashamed of me and this degrading spectacle I have become? But you are me. I am you . . .*

We disparage ourselves endlessly, sometimes with reason (or what seems like a reason), but more often, and more damningly, with a kind of black clarity of judgment that reaches right past all that we have or have not done, reaches past any insight or diagnosis that psychology can offer, and fingers us at the heart of what we are. Wrongness, call it. A stark and utter saturation of self:

> God's most deep decree
> Bitter would have me taste: my taste was me.
> —GERARD MANLEY HOPKINS

Traditionalist Christians call it original sin, I guess, but this seems to me only to take some of the sting off of it—it becomes collective rather than the cold and total loneliness that it is; it also situates the feeling in a social/religious (for some, even historical) context, when a large part of its terror is its inexplicability, its sourcelessness. If only the judgment *were* a "deep decree": that would give it form and potential meaning. But it emerges out of and is defined by blankness, meaninglessness.

How startling, then, to think of Christ experiencing some version of this. And not simply Christ: God. As if all creation had this same corruption in it, this kink in the very grain of things, this mutant cell of self-loathing. As if there were some profound and more-than-human fellowship expressed in the lonely, human need for forgiveness:

> My own heart let me more have pity on; let
> Me live to my sad self hereafter kind.
> —GERARD MANLEY HOPKINS

✤ ✤ ✤

It is no blasphemy to say that every man creates the God creating him. We are facets of a work whose finished form we cannot imagine, though our imaginations, aided by grace, are the means—or at least one means—of its completion.

❖ ❖ ❖

So long as faith is something that "withstands" the assaults of reason, experience, secularization, or even simply the slow erosion of
certainty within my own heart and mind; so long as that verb accurately describes the dynamic between my belief and all that seems
to threaten it, then faith is an illusion in me, a dream that weakness
clings to, rather than the truest form and fruition of strength.

❖ ❖ ❖

Silence is the language of faith. Action—be it church or charity,
politics or poetry—is the translation. As with any translation, action is a mere echo of its original, inevitably faded and distorted, especially as it moves farther from its source. There the comparison
ends, though, for while it is true that action degrades that original
silence, and your moments of meditative communion with God can
seem a world away from the chaotic human encounters to which
those moments compel you, it is also true that without these constant
translations into action, that original, sustaining silence begins to be
less powerful, and then less accessible, and then finally impossible.

❖ ❖ ❖

I always have this sense that something is going to resolve my spiritual anxieties once and for all, that one day I'll just relax and be a
believer. I read book after book. I seek out intense experiences in art,
in nature, or in conversations with people I respect and who seem to
rest more securely in their faith than I do. Sometimes it seems that
gains are made, for these things can and do provide relief and in-
struction. But always the anxiety comes back, is the norm from

which faith deviates, if faith is even what you could call these intense but somehow vague and fleeting experiences of God. I keep forgetting, or perhaps simply will not let myself see, what true faith is, its active and outward nature. I should never pray to be at peace in my belief. I should pray only that my anxiety be given peaceful outlets, that I might be the means to a peace that I myself do not feel.

✤ ✤ ✤

When a man's relation to the divine radically changes and his life and mind open in ways he could not have imagined, he is inclined to think of the transformation in terms of progression—from a lower consciousness to a higher one, or from benighted despair to enlightened joy. This is the first mistake. The second is his immediate desire to lift others, particularly those he loves, into this new state of awareness. But faith is not a new life in this sense; it is the old life newly seen. And the test of that sight is that it leads to connections and continuities, not to renunciations and severances. Nothing is more poisonous, both to one's own faith and to one's relationships, than an overeager urge to proselytize, a too-avid grasp of the "truth." No doubt there is the rare Caedmon whose mute tongue is touched into song by the spirit of God, but I think for most of us—for me, certainly—God comes as an annihilating silence, a silence we must *endure* as well as enjoy. To be sure, the injunction to evangelize is upon every believer, but there is a strict hierarchy of effective methods. "Go forth and spread the gospel by every means possible," said Saint Francis to his followers. "If necessary, use words."

✤ ✤ ✤

Religious despair is often a defense against boredom and the daily grind of existence. Lacking intensity in our lives, we say that we are distant from God and then seek to make that distance into an intense experience. It is among the most difficult spiritual ailments to heal, because it is usually wholly illusory. There are definitely times when we must suffer God's absence, when we are called to enter the dark night of the soul in order to pass into some new understanding of God, some deeper communion with him and with all creation. But this is very rare, and for the most part our dark nights of the soul are, in a way that is more pathetic than tragic, wishful thinking. God is not absent. He is everywhere in the world we are too dispirited to love. To feel him—to *find* him—does not usually require that we renounce all worldly possessions and enter a monastery, or give our lives over to some cause of social justice, or create some sort of sacred art, or begin spontaneously speaking in tongues. All too often the task to which we are called is simply to show a kindness to the irritating person in the cubicle next to us, say, or to touch the face of a spouse from whom we ourselves have been long absent, letting grace wake love from our intense, self-enclosed sleep.

✦ ✦ ✦

It became easy to rekindle the flame of lonely anguish, in part because it never went wholly out. The lie in my life was not the flame but the ease with which I turned to it. Pain has its pleasures, not the least of which are its reliability, immediacy, and even, in a strange way, companionability. "Without loneliness I should be more lonely," as Marianne Moore says, "so I keep it."

✦ ✦ ✦

One of the great impoverishments of contemporary Western Christianity, or at least of liberal Protestantism, is its ignorance of, or allergy to, mysticism. I wouldn't go so far as Simone Weil, who once said that mysticism is the *only* avenue to the experience of

God, but I do think that much of any genuine Christian experience is mystical, which is to say that it is timeless, personal, and that it suggests—or, more accurately, brings to fruition—an essential unity between man and God. (Unity, it goes without saying, is not parity.) But Christian mysticism is not *merely* timeless or personal. The supreme mystery of Christianity—the supreme mystery of Christ himself—is the way in which freedom from time is the call of time, freedom from death the call of death. A mystical experience—and by this I mean to include those experiences of spiritual release and transcendence (in nature, in prayer, in art, etc.) that are available to every single person who will prepare himself for and accept them—does not simply result in action; its reality is confirmed only within action. In the Garden of Gethsemane, the night before his death, Jesus is said to have prayed so hard that he sweated blood—a metaphor, I take it, but in any event a suggestion that his experience of God at that moment was what we would call mystical (it's not all harp music and happy rapture, this brush with Beyond). The next day, Jesus was spat upon, beaten, and hammered to a cross—no metaphor, this—because he did not run away when he had the chance and would not answer the charges against him with anything but silence. It is crucial to feel the brutal reality of it, the (seeming) failure of it, the real world to which a real vision was sacrificed.

❖ ❖ ❖

The proof came soon and plain:
Visions were true which quickened her to run
God's barefoot errands in the rocks of Spain
    Beneath its beating sun,
And lock the O of ecstasy within
The tempered consonants of discipline.
—RICHARD WILBUR, FROM "TERESA"

✤ ✤ ✤

"The reason why Catholic tradition is a tradition," writes Thomas Merton, "is because there is only one living doctrine in Christianity: there is nothing new to be discovered." A little bit of death from a thinker who brought the world so much life. *Nothing new to be discovered?* The minute any human or human institution arrogates to itself a singular knowledge of God, there comes into that knowledge a kind of strychnine pride, and it is as if the most animated and vital creature were instantaneously transformed into a corpse. Any belief that does not recognize and adapt to its own erosions rots from within. Only when doctrine itself is understood to be provisional does doctrine begin to take on a more than provisional significance. Truth inheres not in doctrine itself, but in the spirit with which it is engaged, for the spirit of God is always seeking and creating new forms. (To be fair, Merton himself certainly realized this later in his life, when he became interested in merging ideas from Christianity with Buddhism.)

✤ ✤ ✤

Of course, to assert that all doctrine is provisional and in some fundamental way untenable is itself a doctrine, as subject to sterility and vainglory as the rantings of any radio preacher bludgeoning his listeners with Leviticus. One must learn to be in unknowingness without being proud of it.

✤ ✤ ✤

Simone Weil says that "Absence is the form God takes in this world," which, like every profound human conception of God, is at once true and untrue. It is true insofar as God does not appear to us in any form beyond the forms of the world. It is false insofar as it assumes that God is not present in the forms of the world, in ways that require a lifetime of looking and praying to recognize. Weil's genius is to give form to the feeling of lack that leads a person to cry out that this world, however much it is loved, is not enough. Her language energizes absence, charges it—as in fact it is charged—with divine meaning and power, though the phrase also keeps those things implicit and distant. That is her weakness: she assumes we *know* what form or forms God takes and therefore our perceptions of his absence are not simply accurate but, in this life, final. God's absence is an anguish every honest believer feels, but the problem with Weil's statement is that it stops at this anguish, not realizing that God's absence is always a call to his presence. Abundance and destitution are two facets of the one face of God, and to be spiritually alive in the fullest sense is to recall one when we are standing squarely in the midst of the other.

✦ ✦ ✦

But what does that mean, really? What might it look like in an actual life?

Osip Mandelstam, one of the greatest poets of the twentieth century, one of the greatest *minds* of the twentieth century, died in 1938 at the age of forty-seven. He was last seen at a transit camp for political prisoners in Siberia, picking through a garbage heap for food. It was a situation the poet had long foreseen and even actively precipitated. In 1934, with incredible bravery and suicidal foolishness, Mandelstam recited at a literary gathering a newly composed and now-famous poem, later known as "The Stalin Epigram," which turned all the great leader's pomp into a puppet show:

His grubworm clutch, all oil and vile,
His deadweight deadwords, blonk blonk.

Maybe he believed he was among friends, though even friends had begun to watch their words and backs by then. Maybe he believed in his own gift so utterly that he mistook imaginative freedom for actual freedom, the mind's license for the legs'. Maybe he had the saintly sense not to credit safe distinctions between kinds of freedom and—like Dietrich Bonhoeffer before he left New York to return to his beloved and benighted Germany—did only what his own soul bade him do. In any event, someone at that literary gathering in Moscow, someone whose memory was trained in the same way that Mandelstam's was and could recite a poem after hearing it only once, whispered it in the ear of one of Stalin's goons—and that was it. From Moscow to Leningrad to outer exile in Voronezh, Mandelstam and his wife, Nadezhda, lived on the move, subsisting on scraps and hopes, on love and poetry, on fear:

> Come love let us sit together
> In the cramped kitchen breathing kerosene.
> There's fuel enough to forget the weather,
> The knife is ours and the bread is clean.
>
> Come love let us play the game
> Of what to take and when to run,
> Of come with me and come what may
> And holding hands to hold off the sun.

Probably, though, the Epigram only accelerated events that were inevitable. Mandelstam had long been a thorn in Stalin's brain, as was evident in the famous phone call that Stalin made to Boris Pasternak a few months after Stalin had learned of the Epigram. The two men talked for a bit of Mandelstam and his predicament, before Stalin finally asked the question that was the whole point of his call: But is Mandelstam a true "master"—is he a genius? Pasternak, displaying the political instincts that would enable him to survive, said that it wasn't the right question, but really, it was. It was the pure lyric spirit of Mandelstam that Stalin couldn't abide, the existential liberty and largesse, the free-singing soul that, Stalin seemed to sense, would always slip free of the state's nets. People who think poetry has no power have a very limited conception of what power means. Even now, in this corporate country, where presidents do not call up poets on the telephone, some little lyric is eating into the fat heart of money. And even now some portion of Osip Mandelstam's quicksilver spirit gleams and lives in the lines he left behind:

You have stolen my ocean, my swiftness, my soar,
Delivered me to the clutch of uprupturing earth,

And for what?
The mouth still moves though the man cannot.

There's no need to heroize the stand against Stalin, and in fact it's important to know that Mandelstam later recanted and wrote poems and letters whose only aim was to save his life. It doesn't matter. What matters is the man walking the streets of Voronezh in the days before he would disappear, furiously making his last poems in full awareness of the fate that bore down upon him, still astonished at consciousness, its gift, its cost:

And I was alive in the blizzard of the blossoming pear,
Myself I stood in the storm of the bird-cherry tree.
It was all leaflife and starshower, unerring, self-shattering
    power,
And it was all aimed at me.

What is this dire delight flowering fleeing always earth?
What is being? What is truth?

Blossoms rupture and rapture the air,
All hover and hammer,
Time intensified and time intolerable, sweetness raveling
  rot.
It is now. It is not.

VARIETIES OF QUIET

I have tried to learn the language of Christianity but often feel that I have made no progress at all. I don't mean that Christianity doesn't seem to "work" for me, as if its veracity were measured by its specific utility in my own life. I understand that my understanding must be forged and re-formed within the life of God, and dogma is a means of making this happen: the ropes, clips, and toe spikes whereby one descends into the abyss. But I am also a poet, and I feel the falseness—or no, not even that, a certain inaccuracy and slippage, as if the equipment were worn and inadequate—at every step. And that's in the best moments. In the worst, I'm simply wandering through a discount shopping mall of myth, trying to convince myself there's something worth buying.

✦ ✦ ✦

What is the difference between a mystery in which, and by means of which, one's whole spiritual and intellectual being is elated and completed, and a mystery that merely deflates one's spirit and circumvents one's intellect? The latter, you might say, occurs in quotes. Nothing is more frustrating than listening to an inept or unprepared preacher (or poet!) defer to the "mystery" of existence and God when more mystery is the last thing in the world his words need or can bear— nothing, that is, except perhaps plowing through some twelve-volume Teutonic tome explicating every last letter of the laws of God. I begin to think that *anything* that abstracts us from the physical world is "of the devil," as we said in the baked—and sometimes half-baked—plains of West Texas where I was raised, though there we were more inclined to blame Satan for tempting us too close to the sweet stinks of the earth. What I crave—and what I have known, in fugitive instants—is mystery that utterly obliterates reality by utterly inhabiting it, some ultimate insight that is still sight. Heaven is precision.

✢ ✢ ✢

Polished linoleum shone there. Brass taps shone.
The china cups were very white and big—
An unchipped set with sugar bowl and jug.
The kettle whistled. Sandwich and tea scone
Were present and correct. In case it run,
The butter must be kept out of the sun.
And don't be dropping crumbs. Don't tilt your chair.
Don't reach. Don't point. Don't make noise when you stir.

It is Number 5, New Row, Land of the Dead,
Where grandfather is rising from his place
With spectacles pushed back on a clean bald head
To welcome a bewildered homing daughter
Before she even knocks. "What's this? What's this?"
And they sit down in the shining room together.

—SEAMUS HEANEY, FROM "CLEARANCES"

✢ ✢ ✢

Eternity, the idea of it, is a powerful magnet for the mind, but the heart remains unmoved. It is a truism to say that we are never more alive than when we are closest to our deaths. (It is also at times, if said of one whose suffering has swamped his humanity, an obscenity.) Yet under the easy gesture toward this fatal intensity (easy so long as it is safely intellectual, remote from us) there is a sharp edge: it might take an illness for you to feel that edge, either in your body or in the body of one you love, or it might simply be a kind of cut in consciousness so sharp that there is a pause between you and all that is not you, and like a quick-handed cook whose deft slicing suddenly opens his own thumb, you are stuck in the shock of watching.

We live in and by our senses, which are conditioned in and by our deaths. When some singular aspect of reality—an object, a person, even a duration of time—seems to acquire a life in excess of itself, what we feel is more complicated than joy. This is because that excess is at once some inexplicable ongoingness of the thing and the loss of the thing as it is, at once eternity and oblivion. And this is why poetry is so powerful, and so integral to any unified spiritual life: it preserves both aspects of spiritual experience, because to name is to praise and lose in one instant. So many ways of saying God.

✤ ✤ ✤

At the alder-darkened brink
Where the stream slows to a lucid jet
I lean to the water, dinting its top with sweat,
And see, before I can drink,

A startled inchling trout
Of spotted near-transparency,
Trawling a shadow solider than he.
He swerves now, darting out

To where, in a flicked slew
Of sparks and glittering silt, he weaves
Through stream-bed rocks, disturbing foundered leaves,
And butts then out of view

Beneath a sliding glass
Crazed by the skimming of a brace
Of burnished dragon-flies across its face,
In which deep cloudlets pass

And a white precipice
Of mirrored birch-trees plunges down
Toward where the azures of the zenith drown.
How shall I drink all this?

Joy's trick is to supply
Dry lips with what can cool and slake,
Leaving them dumbstruck also with an ache
Nothing can satisfy.

—RICHARD WILBUR, "HAMLEN BROOK"

✦ ✦ ✦

"God is distant, difficult," writes Geoffrey Hill, a contemporary religious poet whose work—distant, difficult—might be said to have grown out of the seed of that assumption. But in fact distance from God—the assumption of it—is often not the terror and scourge we make it out to be, but the very opposite: it is false comfort, for it asks nothing immediate of us, or what it asks is interior, intellectual, self-enclosed. The result is a moment of meditative communion, perhaps, or a work of art, or even—O my easy, hazy God—one more little riff on the Ineffable.

To believe in—to serve—Christ, on the other hand, is quite difficult, and precisely because of how near he is to us at all times. In Seattle once, when I was twenty-one and working at some crap temp job downtown, I used to spend my lunch hours near the docks. One particular day when everything was crisp, blue, new—and even the molten men emerging from the metal with which they were working, and the bickering gulls buoyed up in gusts, and my own release from numbing office efficiency seemed to verge on some mysterious, tremendous articulation of light and time—suddenly a tattered, gangrenous man staggered toward me with his arms out like a soul in hell.

Modern spiritual consciousness is predicated upon the fact that God is gone, and spiritual experience, for many of us, amounts mostly to an essential, deeply felt and necessary, but ultimately inchoate and transitory feeling of oneness or unity with existence. It is mystical and valuable, but distant. Christ, though, is a shard of glass in your gut. Christ is God crying *I am here*, and here not only in what exalts and completes and uplifts you, but here in what appalls, offends, and degrades you, here in what activates and exacerbates all that you would call not-God. To walk through the fog of God toward the clarity of Christ is difficult because of how unlovely, how "ungodly" that clarity often turns out to be.

I thrust my lunch into that man's hands, one of which was furred green as if a mold were growing on it, and fled.

✤ ✤ ✤

It is easy enough to write and talk about God while remaining comfortable within the contemporary intellectual climate. Even people who would call themselves unbelievers often use the word gesturally, as a ready-made synonym for mystery. But if nature abhors a vacuum, Christ abhors a vagueness. If God is love, Christ is love for this one person, this one place, this one time-bound and time-ravaged self. Geoffrey Hill:

> What is there in my heart that you should sue
> so fiercely for its love? What kind of care
> brings you as though a stranger to my door
> through the long night and in the icy dew

seeking the heart that will not harbor you,
that keeps itself religiously secure?
                    —FROM "LACHRIMAE AMANTIS"

Religiously secure. A brilliant phrase, and not simply because it suggests the radical lack of security, the disruption of ordinary life that a turn toward Christ entails, but also this: for some people, and probably for all people for some of the time, religion, church, the whole essential but secondary edifice that has grown out of primary spiritual experience—all this is the last place in the world where they are going to find God, who is calling for them in the everyday voices of other people, other sufferings and celebrations, or simply in the cellular soul of what *is*:

> Centaury with your staunch bloom
> you there alder beech you fern
> midsummer closeness my far home,
> fresh traces of lost origin.

> Silvery the black cherries hang,
> the plum-tree oozes through each cleft
> and horse-flies siphon the green dung,
> glued to the sweetness of their graft:

> immortal transience, a "kind
> of otherness," self-understood,
> BE FAITHFUL grows upon the mind
> as lichen glimmers on the wood.
>   —GEOFFREY HILL, FROM "TWO
>   CHORAL-PRELUDES"

❖ ❖ ❖

And yet the merely individual connection with the divine, that moment of supernatural communion that occurs at the end of "Two Choral-Preludes" above, the whole modern muddle of gauzy ontologies and piecemeal belief that leads so many people to dismiss all doctrine out of hand, or to say that they are spiritual but not religious, or to emphasize some form of individual "transcendence" over other aspects of spiritual experience—all this is fine until life, or death, comes crashing into you with its all-too-specific terrors and sufferings. We do not need definite beliefs because their objects are necessarily true. We need them because they enable us to stand on steady spots from which the truth may be glimpsed. And not simply glimpsed—because certainly revelation is available outside of dogma; indeed all dogma, if it's alive at all, is the result of revelation at one time or another—but gathered in. Definite beliefs are what make the radical mystery—those moments when we suddenly *know* there is a God, about whom we "know" absolutely nothing—accessible to us and our ordinary, unmysterious lives. And more crucially: definite beliefs enable us to withstand the storms of suffering that come into every life, and that tend to destroy any spiritual disposition that does not have deep roots.

✢ ✢ ✢

Of course I say all this as someone who gets so bored in church that I often recite poems to myself in my head, someone an interviewer once called (approvingly, I think) an "atheist Christian," someone who all too often forgets that it is much more important to assert and lay claim to the God that you believe in rather than forever drawing the line at the doctrine you don't. But I say it, too, as someone who has had his own gauzy ontology overwhelmed with real blood, my mystical sense of God-in-nature obliterated by nature wreaking havoc with my body. If wisdom is, as Kant said, "organized life," I'm afraid I have little to offer. I am still right down in the filthy tumult. If I ever sound like a preacher in these passages, it's only because I have a hornet's nest of voluble and conflicting parishioners inside of me.

❖ ❖ ❖

Does the decay of belief among educated people in the West precede the decay of language used to define and explore belief, or do we find the fire of belief fading in us only because the words are sodden with overuse and imprecision, and will not burn? We need a poetics of belief, a language capacious enough to include a mystery that, ultimately, defeats it, and sufficiently intimate and inclusive to serve not only as individual expression but as communal need. I sometimes think that this transformation is already happening outside of religious institutions, that faith is remaking itself in the work of contemporary artists and thinkers (yes, I mean to deflect the agency like that: the moment an artist becomes conscious of remaking or reimagining faith, he becomes a barrier to it). For twenty-five years I have held this passage from Marilynne Robinson's novel *Housekeeping* in my mind:

> Imagine a Carthage sown with salt, and all the sowers gone, and the seeds lain however long in the earth, till there rose finally in vegetable profusion leaves and trees of rime and brine. What flowering would there be in such a garden? Light would force each salt calyx to open in prisms, and to fruit heavily with bright globes of water—peaches and grapes are little more than that, and where the world was salt there would be greater need of slaking. For need can blossom into all the compensations it requires. To crave and to have are as like as a thing and its shadow. For when does a berry break upon the tongue as sweet as when one longs to taste it, and when is the taste refracted into so many hues and savors of ripeness and earth, and when do our senses know any thing so utterly as when we lack it? And here again is a foreshadowing—the world

will be made whole. For to wish for a hand on one's hair is all but to feel it. So whatever we may lose, very craving gives it back to us again. Though we dream and hardly know it, longing, like an angel, fosters us, smooths our hair, and brings us wild strawberries.

This seemed (and seems) to me, besides being prose of consummate clarity and beauty, to so perfectly articulate not only the sense of absence that for years I felt permeating every spiritual aspect of my life, but also, and more important, to bestow upon it an energy and agency, a prayerful but indefinable promise: "the world will be made whole." The language is clearly biblical, but it occurs in a secular context; it is spiritually suggestive (and useful) but rooted in— even contingent upon—the actual natural world; it is absolutely given over to the transitory instant that, by means of its intense attentiveness, it transcends.

People flocked to the book, especially—if my conversations over the years are any indication—secular readers, most of whom seem not to have even noticed the Christian dimensions of the language and the story. I'm not sure the book offered much of a way forward— its ending has always seemed to me the least convincing part of the novel—but it cleared the metaphysical air, so to speak; it gave us— would-be believers, haunted unbelievers, determined secularists whose very passion for the book undermined their iron exteriors— something to build on.

And then: twenty-four years of silence. There were radiant articles here and there, and a book of essays, but no more fiction. I wondered if Robinson had simply lost her faith in the form, and like many people I was surprised and pleased when, in 2004, she published *Gilead*, a novel told from the perspective of a mid-twentieth-century midwestern Protestant preacher who is old and dying. The book reads like a flowering of the emptiness and absence, the whole bone-cold weather of elegy, that both animated and limited *Housekeeping*. ("Limited" in terms of what the book could do for a person;

in the end, I feel that *Housekeeping* is Robinson's best book.) There are even passages in both books that echo and answer each other, such as the one above and this:

> I feel sometimes as if I were a child who opens its eyes on the world once and sees amazing things it will never know any names for and then has to close its eyes again. I know this is all mere apparition compared to what awaits us, but it is only lovelier for that. There is a human beauty in it. And I can't believe that, when we have all been changed and put on incorruptibility, we will forget our fantastic condition of mortality and impermanence, the great bright dream of procreating and perishing that meant the whole world to us. In eternity this world will be Troy, I believe, and all that has passed here will be the epic of the universe, the ballad they sing in the streets. Because I don't imagine any reality putting this one in the shade entirely, and I think piety forbids me to try.

The specifically Christian element is more explicit here (she alludes to First Corinthians: "We shall not all be taken, but we shall all be changed"), but it's a kind of Christianity that would be unfamiliar to many people, including many Christians. If piety forbids one to imagine any afterlife that makes this life seem altogether inferior, then piety essentially forbids one from imagining any afterlife at all. (Unless you simply imagine this life somehow continuing in perpetuity, which would, even for the happiest person out there, eventually be a kind of hell.) One can still have *faith* in an afterlife, but it is a faith both kindled and confined by the earth. What, according to *Housekeeping*, does our most intense longing for otherness, our soul's notion of some ultimate elsewhere, finally bring us? The wild strawberries that are right in front of our eyes.

✤ ✤ ✤

It is enough in literature—it is essential—to keep one's little patch of language pure, to reconcile oneself to nothing that has not passed through the crucible of one's own most intense experiences and thoughts. But that won't do for life, or faith, which are defined by, and contained within, relationships. And to be in a relationship often means forgoing the self and its crucible of "truth," learning to live with—and love—the very things that compromise our notions of what we need, what we think, what we are. I feel a strong need—an imperative, really—to believe something in common; indeed, I feel that any belief I have that is not in some way shared is probably just the workings of my own ego, a common form of modern idolatry.

✧ ✧ ✧

The soul at peace—the mystic, the poet working well—is not simply inclined to silence but inclined to valorize it. Poets say that the better part of poetry is what is not said; mystics and other meditative savants say that the final fruition of prayer is silence. And they are correct. And yet the soul in extremity craves language; and even more than that, craves within language some fixed point of perception, some articulation of soul and circumstance that neither wavers nor decays, some—how the modern mind pretzels itself trying not to speak this one word—truth. But here's a "truth": every word, even "the," begins to leak meaning the minute you turn your attention to it. When I was young, until I got sick in fact, what I most wanted from art was to tease those implications and connotations out, to lose myself in, fuse myself with, the larger meaning that this constant loss of meaning makes possible. But now what I crave is writing that strives to erase implications, art that aspires to get right down to the nub of Now. I want the "pure, clear word," as James Wright once called it: thought and object, mind and matter soldered seamlessly together by pain, faith, grief, grace. That I don't believe in such a word only intensifies my desire for it.

✢ ✢ ✢

When life is thriving in us, we crave to get beyond it: experience that takes us out of ourselves, poetry that articulates a shape and space for the inexpressible, prayer that obliterates self-consciousness for the sake of God. When it is death that is thriving in us, though, when the inexpressible has begun to seep into us like some last, ineluctable dusk, and the tick of each instant is the click of a door closing us out—we look back. Hospitalized again, breathless because of my useless blood, tethered twenty-four hours a day to multiple chemotherapies, angered into someone I hardly recognize and do not like, I reach over randomly to the pile of despised books on the bedstand and read

> Terrifying are the attent sleek thrushes on the lawn,
> More coiled steel than living—a poised
> Dark deadly eye, those delicate legs
> Triggered to stirrings beyond sense—with a start, a bounce, a stab
> Overtake the instant and drag out some writhing thing.
>
> —TED HUGHES, "THRUSHES"

and weep for the world this tiny, terrifying, and blessedly untranscendental clarity gives back to me again.

✢ ✢ ✢

Too many elegies
elevating

sadness
to a kind

of sad
religion:

one wants
in the end

just once
to befriend

one's own
loneliness,

to make
of the ache

of inwardness . . .
something—

music maybe,
or even just believing

in it,
and summer,

and the long room
alone

where the child
chances

on a bee
banging

against one
pane

like an attack
of happiness.

✦ ✦ ✦

Saint Augustine's famous phrase at the end of his endless book on the Trinity: "We have said this not in order to have said something, but in order not to have remained altogether silent." How many theologians have I heard quote this self-justifying sentence, as if the only alternative were between a kind of iron-willed industriousness and impotent silence. Augustine isn't to blame (elsewhere he says, "If you think you have understood God, it is not God"), but contemporary interpretations of that one sentence should be balanced by another famous quotation, this one from Wittgenstein: "Whereof one cannot speak, thereof one must be silent." The purpose of theology—the purpose of any thinking about God—is to make the silences clearer and starker to us, to make the unmeaning—by which I mean those aspects of the divine that will not be reduced to human meanings—more irreducible and more terrible, and thus ultimately more wonderful. This is why art is so often better at theology than theology is.

✦ ✦ ✦

The great battle that Augustine faces is with his own physical desires. His total commitment to God is simultaneous with a sharp renunciation of lust (or, more accurately, an acceptance of the grace that enables his will toward God to vanquish his will for physical pleasure). But what in the world can this mean for a modern person with some notion of biology, or just a sense that God is not some puritanical schoolmarm? Was Augustine, then, who was one of the greatest thinkers of the Western world, simply blinkered in this sense, a little simplistic? It seems a lot easier to posit a concrete thing between ourselves and God, a specific and potentially eradicable sin, than to live in the mental storm of modern faith, in which faith itself is always *the* issue. Renouncing sex may not be easier than renouncing disbelief, but at least you can understand it; it is a problem you can, so to speak, grapple with. Trying to take hold of disbelief is like fighting your own shadow.

Or is it? Here's a quote from Augustine, describing the extended and anguishing time when the call of God and his own lust were at war within him:

> But I was immobilized—less by another's static imposition than by my own static will. For the enemy had in thrall my power to choose, which he had used to make a chain for binding me. From bad choices an urge arises; and the urge, yielded to, becomes a compulsion; and the compulsion, unresisted, becomes a slavery— each link in this process connected with the others, which is why I call it a chain—and that chain had a tyrannical grip around me. The new will I felt stirring in me, a will to "give you free worship" and enjoy what I yearned for, my God, my only reliable happiness, could not break away from the will made strong by long dominance. Two wills were mine, old and new, of the flesh, of the spirit, each warring on the other, and between their dissonances was my soul disintegrating.

The object of idolatry is not really the point here. It is the war of wills that any genuine spiritual experience—and you will know such an experience is genuine by the extent to which it demands uncomfortable change—sets off inside the heart and mind of the one who has it. Every man has a man within him who must die. For Augustine that man was the one whose spiritual being was occluded by his physical being. For me—and I suspect for many modern believers, or would-be believers—the problem is not physical, but nevertheless more palpable than we allow ourselves to admit, and the tension within us that seems so urgently and singularly "modern" is in fact the oldest sin in the Book: intellectual pride.

✦ ✦ ✦

> One thing remained attainable, close and unlost amidst all the losses: language. Language was not lost, in spite of all that happened. But it had to go through its own responselessness, go through horrible silences, go through the thousand darknesses of death-bringing speech.

Paul Celan. Who lost both his parents in the Holocaust and spent time himself inside a labor camp. Who found a way to write poetry—a whole new kind of poetry—after events so cataclysmic and depraved that the act of making art in their wake seemed, to many, not merely an impertinence but an obscenity. God was gone, and not simply in an intellectual sense either, not in the God-is-dead style of coffee-shop existentialists, but really gone, ripped from humanity's very viscera, a howling silence at the center of some of the worst suffering men and women have known. This would seem to be the end of theology, and for some theologians, it was. For others, though, it was, as for Celan, a hard new beginning:

> Our faith begins at the point where atheists suppose that it must be at an end. Our faith begins with the bleakness and power which is the night of the cross, abandonment, temptation and doubt about everything that exists! Our faith must be born where it is abandoned by all tangible reality; it must be born of nothingness,

it must taste this nothingness and be given it to taste in a way that
no philosophy of nihilism can imagine.

—H. J. IWAND

I take the quote from Jürgen Moltmann's great book *The Crucified God*. Moltmann, as it happens, was a conscripted low-level German soldier and a contemporary of Celan's. He had no experience
of Christianity until he converted in an Allied prison camp, where
he also first learned of the horrors that the Nazis had done—horrors
that, if he had not exactly been fighting for (he surrendered to the
first Allied soldier he saw), were nonetheless done by his country and
in his name. Moltmann, who compared his experience of Christ in
the POW camp to Christ's merciful descent into hell ("I didn't find
Christ, he found me"), forcefully asserts the presence and power of
the living God, but his work is haunted by the same question that
haunts Celan's: How does theology exist after—how does it speak
to—such suffering? For Moltmann the answer lay in that moment
on the cross when Christ agonizes *My God, my God, why hast thou
forsaken me?*, and he argued in *The Crucified God* that all modern
theology had to be developed "in earshot of the dying Christ."

It's not difficult to see how the language of poetry was changed
by Celan, whose poems are full of jagged fragments and lacunae,
austerities and poverties, words crammed roughly together so that
meanings splinter off wildly as from a wreck—and then, through it
all, miraculously, a sable radiance:

Noone kneads us again from earth and loam,
noone evokes our dust.
Noone.

Praised be you, noone.
Because of you we wish
to bloom.

Against
you.

A nothing
were we, are we, will
we be, blossoming:
the nothing's—, the noonesrose.

With
its pistil soulbright,
its stamen heavencrazed,
its crown red
from the purpleword that we sang
over, o over
its thorn.

—"PSALM," TRANSLATED
BY CID CORMAN

That's one thing Celan teaches: to pray one's hate ("Praised be you, noone . . ."). But to despise implies something *to* despise, and so, in their own angry way, these black psalms sing God back into being.

But how does the language of faith change? One of my problems with Christianity is that all talk of heaven seems absurd to me, though I believe that we have souls and that they survive our deaths, in some sense that we are entirely incapable of imagining ("Imagine a Carthage sown with salt . . ."). I don't know what it means to say that Christ "died for my sins" (who wants that? who invented that perverse calculus?), but I do understand—or intuit, rather—the notion of God not above or beyond or immune to human suffering, but in the very midst of it, intimately with us in our sorrow, our sense of abandonment, our hellish astonishment at finding ourselves utterly alone, utterly helpless.

How to speak of these things? Language, even as it reaches for a life beyond this one, must bear the mark of being lost. Not having been lost. Being lost. Because however intently one believes in the resurrection, it remains a matter *of* belief. That absolute destitution and longing that caused Christ to call out on the cross, though, that terror and emptiness in the presence of death and grief—these things we know, this reality is the ground on which we can begin to build. Or rebuild:

Christians who do not have the feeling that they must flee the crucified Christ have probably not yet understood him in a sufficiently radical way . . . More radical Christian faith can only mean committing oneself without reserve to the "crucified God." This is dangerous. It does not promise the confirmation of one's own conceptions, hopes and good intentions. It promises first of all the pain of repentance and fundamental change. It offers no recipe for success. But it brings a confrontation with the truth. It is not positive and constructive, but is in the first instance critical and destructive. It does not bring man into a better harmony with himself and his environment, but into contradiction with himself and his environment . . . The "religion of the cross," if faith on this basis can ever be so called, does not elevate and edify in the usual sense, but scandalizes; and most of all it scandalizes one's "coreligionists" in one's own circle. But by this scandal, it brings liberation into a world which is not free. For ultimately, in a civilization which is constructed on the principle of achievement and enjoyment, and therefore makes pain and death a private matter, excluded from its public life . . . there is nothing so unpopular as for the crucified God to be made a present reality through faith. It alienates alienated men, who have come to terms with alienation.

—JÜRGEN MOLTMANN, *THE CRUCIFIED GOD*

✦ ✦ ✦

We want to fill what wants to be empty; we seek meaning in what seeks to be free of that. Everything is aspiration, effort, achievement, though the true goal is often immune to all of this, sometimes even anathema to it. The great Polish poet Zbigniew Herbert has a poem in which, after a lifetime of aspiring to the stars, the speaker finally sees them fall right down the sky in terror at being his everything. And then?

> he no longer dreams of flight
> but of a fall
> that draws like lightning
> a profile of infinity
> —FROM "CHOSEN BY THE STARS," TRANSLATED
> BY JOHN AND BOGDANA CARPENTER

A beautiful new expression of an old idea. George Herbert, in the sixteenth century: "Then shall the fall further the flight in me." This isn't simply the literary equivalent of "bottoming out" before you can begin to recover. No, what both Herberts are pointing to here is the fact that sometimes meaning inheres in unmeaning. I don't mean "what seems like unmeaning"; this is hedging one's bets, as if meaning were always there waiting to be found, as if meaning-lessness were a veil we need only learn to tear aside. It is the absolute-ness of meaninglessness that Christianity, as I understand it, inhabits and inflects, the shock and stark violence of the cross that discloses the living Christ. Revelation, like creation, arises not merely out of nothingness but *by means of it*.

There is a long-muted but recently resurgent tradition in Christianity that seeks not to articulate exactly, but to frame a space in language wherein this dynamic between meaning and meaningless-ness, or between God and the absence of God, can occur. "We pray to God to free us of God," Meister Eckhart writes, suggesting, I think, that we pray to God to free us from the ways in which we pray to and understand God; we pray in language to be lifted out of the limitations of language. Or there is this, from the thirteenth-century beguine Marguerite Porete:

> I call this life clear because she has surmounted the blindness of the life of annihilation . . . She does not know who she is, God or humankind. For she is not, but God knows of himself in her for her of himself. Such a Lady does not seek God. She has no "of what" with which to do that. She need not do that. For what would she seek then?

The "of what" that Porete mentions, according to Michael Sells in his book *Mystical Languages of Unsaying*, refers to the questioning will, the ever active part of our minds that will not stop asking "why." This is what, when God expresses himself in us—and when we come as close as possible to expressing this state in language—is gone. Sells points out how close this passage is to Sufi thought:

> The fundamental doctrine of Sufism is the annihilation (*fanā'*) and subsequent abiding (*baqā'*) of the self. These mystical states are compared to a polished mirror. When the heart of the Sufi is "polished" and the ego-self of the Sufi passes away, the divine is said to reveal to it(self) through it(self) its mystery; or to use a different convention, to reveal to Him/him through Him/him His/his mystery. At this point the referential distinction between reflexive and nonreflexive, self and other, human and divine, breaks down.

Apophatic language, language that seems to negate or undermine the very assertions that it is making, may be at this point not simply the only "proper" means of addressing or invoking God, but the only efficacious one as well. "O Lord, let me not love Thee, if I love Thee not," writes George Herbert. We need to be shocked out of our easy acceptance of—or our facile resistance to—propositional language about God. Besides being useless as any definitive description of God, such language is simply not adequate for the intense and sacred spiritual turmoil that so many contemporary people feel.

❖ ❖ ❖

It goes both ways, though: mystical experience needs some form of dogma in order not to dissipate into moments of spiritual intensity that are merely personal, and dogma needs regular infusions of unknowingness to keep from calcifying into the predictable, pontificating, and anti-intellectual services so common in mainstream American churches. So what does all this mean practically? It means that congregations must be conscious of the persistent and ineradicable loneliness that makes a person seek communion, with other people and with God, in the first place. It means that conservative churches that are infused with the bouncy brand of American optimism one finds in sales pitches are selling shit. It means that liberal churches that go months without mentioning the name of Jesus, much less the dying Christ, have no more spiritual purpose or significance than a local union hall. It means that we—those of us who call ourselves Christians—need a revolution in the way we worship. This could mean many different things—poetry as liturgy, focused and extended silences, learning from other religious traditions and rituals (this seems crucial), incorporating apophatic language. But one thing it means for sure: we must be conscious of language as language, must call into question every word we use until we refine or remake a language that is fit for our particular religious doubts and despairs—and of course (and most of all!) our joys.

❖ ❖ ❖

What is it about speaking faith that releases it? That almost creates it at times, when faith has fallen so far into the rut of habit or been rendered so mute by despair? At a reading at a hip loft space full of hip literary people I keep dropping God into every segue, keep needing the poems to be heard in that context, even the ones that work better without it. Public proselytizing does little good, at least in words, and I've never felt a call (or competence) in that direction anyway. No, it's more that the occasion is calling forth my primal voice, poetry, and in that voice, thank God, is God. There is risk in it, and a raw awkwardness, and only now, as my soul seems to stir inside of me, do I begin to feel faith's latency echoing back down the days through which I walked—I thought—faithlessly, giving those days shape and dimension, giving me reason to have lived them. The feeling is akin to—but not the same as—the feeling I had when writing the poems in the first place, a pure charge of electric life that so illuminates a moment that the past shines by means of it and the future seems possible.

❖ ❖ ❖

Faith is nothing more—but how much this is—than a motion of the soul toward God. It is not belief. Belief has objects—Christ was resurrected, God created the earth—faith does not. Even the motion of faith is mysterious and inexplicable: I say the soul moves "toward" God, but that is only the limitation of language. It may be God who moves, the soul that opens for him. Faith is faith in the soul. Faith is the word "faith" decaying into pure meaning.

❖ ❖ ❖

And yet, and yet . . . Saint Bonaventure:

> There are three crossings, that is, the crossing that is a beginning (incipientium) and the crossing that is in the making (profi-

cientium) and the crossing that is an arrival (pervenientium) . . . this then is the threefold paschal crossing, of which the first is through the sea of contrition, the second through the desert of religion, the third through the Jordan of death; and thus we arrive at the promised land.

The *desert* of religion: as if we moderns had a lock on institutional contempt, as if we were the only ones suspicious of our desire to codify the way to God. Bonaventure was writing in the thirteenth century. His metaphor for the church's part in achieving grace is hardly hopeful; it is however immutable. You cannot go around a desert. And once you're in, once you've turned at all to God, then you are stuck with the language and rituals of whatever faith you know. Like it or not, religion rises between the man of God—or the man who would be of God if he could believe in him—and his death.

✤ ✤ ✤

From the start I had a great desire to change the language, for example, to replace the word "grace" with something else. I was annoyed by the word "humility" and many other words, which I hadn't used in a long while. It seemed to me that "faith" was also a matter for the dictionary. Of course, language is a system of metaphors and contains the whole experience of farming communities, migrant peoples, various social orders, monarchy, slavery, serfdom. We've grown used to many words, forgetting that they're only metaphors, though in their own time they were actively metaphoric, new discoveries. I thought that ceaseless linguistic invention was required even in the realm of faith. Thinkers must be poets.

I'm slowly relinquishing my claims in linguistic matters, though, and I humbly return to faith and to humility, since these are word-vessels so saturated with content through ages of thought and use that to abandon them would be the act of a heedless parvenu.

—ANNA KAMIEŃSKA, *DIARIES*

She's right. You can't really know a religion from the outside, and you can't simply "re-create" it to your liking. That is to say, you can know everything about a religion—its history, iconography, scripture, etc.—but all of that will remain intellectual, mere information, so long as your own soul is not at risk. To have faith in a religion, any religion, is to accept at some primary level that its particular language of words and symbols says something true about reality. This doesn't mean that the words and symbols *are* reality (that's fundamentalism), nor that you will ever master those words and symbols well enough to regard reality as some fixed thing. What it does mean, though, is that "you can no more be religious in general than you can speak language in general" (George Lindbeck), and that the only way to deepen your knowledge and experience of ultimate divinity is to deepen your knowledge and experience of the all-too-temporal symbols and language of a particular religion. Lindbeck would go so far as to say that the religion you grew up with has such a bone-deep hold on you that, as with a native language, it's your only hope for true religious fluency. I wouldn't go that far, as I have friends whose patchwork religious lives have a hard-earned authenticity to them. I do think, though, that regardless of what religion one practices, eventually one has to submit to certain symbols and language that may be inadequate in order to have those inadequacies transcended. There is an analogue with poetry here: you can't spend your whole life questioning whether language can represent reality. At some point you have to believe that the inadequacies of the words you use will be transcended by the faith with which you use them. You have to believe that poetry has some reach into reality itself, or you have to go silent.

✦ ✦ ✦

Exhortations to myself, mostly. My restless, useless parishioners. For the question remains: What do you do, what do you say, what in the world are you going to *believe in* when you are dying? It is not enough to act *as if* when the wave is closing over you, and that little whiff of the ineffable you get from meditation or mysticism is toxic to the dying man, who needs the rock of one real truth. I have spent so much time in the hospital recently, and so much time in truly perilous situations, yet never have I felt farther from any adequate prayer. A preacher comes to see me, and we sit like stiff antagonists because the language either won't come out of my mouth, or feels so foreign, so obviously a capitulation, so—I should just say it—*embarrassing* to me, that I basically do a little linguistic dance around Christianity, as if I were hedging my bets. Is it merely, right to the bitter end, a form of intellectual pride? No, it's more serious than that. There is some disconnect between language and life. I cannot live toward these words—grace, sin, salvation—with the same creative abandon that poetry makes possible in me. Or perhaps I should say that I simply cannot *live* with the same creative abandon with which I can (sometimes) write, because life is a hell of a lot more difficult—and important—than art. And thus I cannot live up to my own exhortations and am left with my parvenu hesitations, my lonely and vertiginous mysticisms, sounding not the clear, true notes of what I believe, but the varieties of quiet in between.

✦ ✦ ✦

Varieties
of quiet

I quote
from a poet

no one knows.
And no one

knows
me too

if by chance
happening

here
some far year

when I am
not:

it matters
I tell you

it matters
the matter

one mind
collects,

one memory
protects

when memory's
kin

to that wordless
feeling

words
open in your head:

*varieties
of quiet*

*varieties
of quiet*

There are many
friend

as many
as the dead.

MORTIFY OUR WOLVES

There comes a moan to the cancer clinic. There comes a sound so low and unvarying it seems hardly human, more a note the wind might strike off jags of rock and ice in some wasted place too remote for anyone to hear.

We hear, and look up as one at the two attendants hurriedly wheeling something so shrunken it seems merely another rumple in the blanket, tubes traveling in and out of its impalpability, its only life this lifeless cry.

The doors open soundlessly and the pall of sorrow goes flowing off into the annihilating brightness beyond. Then the doors close and we as one look down, not meeting each other's eyes, and wait.

✤ ✤ ✤

The terrible thing—it could perhaps be a glorious thing, always the ill are meant to see it as such, are reproached if they don't (carpe fucking diem)—the terrible thing about feeling the inevitability of your own early death is the way it colors every single scene. At some friends' house I am moved by the beauty and antics of their two-year-old daughter—moved, and then saddened to think of the daughter D. and I might have, for whom my death will be some deep, lightless hole that for the rest of her life she will walk around, grief the very ground of her being. What is this world that we are so at odds with, this beauty by which we are so wounded, and into which God has so utterly gone?

✣ ✣ ✣

Into which, rather than *from* which: in a grain of grammar, a world of hope.

✣ ✣ ✣

That conversions often happen after or during intense life experiences, especially traumatic experiences, is sometimes used as evidence against them. The sufferer isn't in his right mind. The mind, tottering at the abyss of despair or death, shudders back toward any simplicity, any coherency it can grasp, and the man calls out to God. Never mind that the God that comes at such moments may not be simple at all, arises out of and includes the very abyss the man would flee. Never mind that in traumatic experience many people *lose* their faith—or what looked like faith?—rather than find it. It is the flinch from life—which, the healthy are always quick to remind us, includes death—and the flight to God that cannot be trusted.

But how could it be otherwise? It takes a real jolt to get us to change our jobs, our relationships, our daily coffee consumption, for goodness' sake—or, if we are wired that way, to change our addiction to change. How much more urgency is needed, how much more primal fear, to startle the heart out of its ruts and ruins? It's true that God comes to the prophet Elijah not in the whirlwind, and not in the earthquake, and not in the fire that follows, but in the "still, small voice" that these ravages make plain. But the very wording of that passage makes it clear that the voice, though finally more powerful than the ravages it follows, is not altogether apart from them. That voice is always there, and for everyone. For some of us, unfortunately, it takes terror and pain to make us capable of hearing it.

✤ ✤ ✤

Once more, years between that last entry and this one. Years of working on these little fragments here and there, finding God here and there among the ongoing delights and demolitions of daily life. Years of treatments, abatements, hope, hell. I have a cancer that is as rare as it is unpredictable, "smoldering" in some people for decades, turning others to quick tinder. I also now have two children, two lovely, live-wire, and preternaturally alert little girls who were born within eight minutes of each other, at a time when it seemed as if the cancer had been driven away by drugs so futuristic I couldn't get past my amazement to feel much fear, and with so few side effects that it seemed I would be able to take them forever. That hasn't proved to be the case.

Though people never say it, you can see it in their eyes sometimes, the question: How could you do it? How could you bring children into a situation so precarious? How could you seed them with this grief? And of course we ask ourselves these questions, my wife and I, when things are bad with me or difficult at home. But then we see them offering each other flowers they've picked from the backyard, or stopping amid their madcap play to kiss each other, or, when we walk into their nursery in the mornings, throwing back their heads and laughing like little palpable fruitions of the love that first led us out of ourselves and to each other—we see these things and we ask: How could we *not* have had them? How could they not be? How could such life, such love, ever have remained latent and dormant within us?

✤ ✤ ✤

Part of the mystery of grace is the way it operates not only as present joy and future hope, but also retroactively, in a way: the past is suffused with a presence that, at the time, you could only feel as the most implacable absence. This is why being saved (I dislike the language too, not because it's inaccurate but because it's corrupted by contemporary usage, a hands-in-the-air-holy-seizure sort of rapture, a definitive sense of rift) involves embracing rather than renouncing one's past. It is true that Christ makes a man anew, that there is some ultimate change in him. But part of that change is the ability to see your life as a whole, to feel the form and unity of it, to become a creature made for and assimilated into existence, rather than a desperate, fragmented man striving against existence or caught forever just outside of it.

❖ ❖ ❖

Though I have in my life experienced gout, bladder stones, a botched bone marrow biopsy, and various other screamable insults, until recently I had no idea what pain was. It islands you. You sit there in your little skeletal constriction of self—of disappearing self—watching everyone you love, however steadfastly they may remain by your side, drift farther and farther away. There is too much cancer packed into my bone marrow, which is inflamed and expanding, creating pressure outward on the bones. "Bones don't like to stretch," a doctor tells me. Indeed. It is in my legs mostly, but also up in one shoulder and in my face. It is a dull, devouring pain, as if the earth were already—but slowly—eating me. And then, with a wrong move or simply a shift in breath, it is a lightning strike of absolute feeling and absolute oblivion fused in one flash. Mornings I make my way out of bed very early and, after taking all the pain medicine I can take without dying, sit on the couch and try to make myself small by bending over and holding my ankles. And I pray. Not to God, though, who also seems to have abandoned this island, but to the pain. That it ease up ever so little, that it let me breathe. That it not—but I know it will—get worse.

✤ ✤ ✤

Poetry has its uses for despair. It can carve a shape for pain; it can give one's loss a form and dimension that it might *be* loss and not simply a hopeless haunting. It can do these things for one person, or it can do them for an entire culture. But poetry is for psychological, spiritual, or emotional pain. For physical pain it is, like everything but drugs, useless.

✤ ✤ ✤

On Thursdays the painlady leans toward me, gleaning pain. She is precise, sharp shouldered, soft-spoken—as a painlady should be. I am emaciated, palsied, hostile, hopeful in the shamefaced way of hopeless people. We have by now tried many things, but there is always some new patch or pill up her sleeve. She is a famous pain-lady, I gather, and has been in Libya for a conference, or in Brazil for a conference, here and there—where is there not pain? Excretion, sexual function, depression's oily entropy: she runs down the side effects without embarrassment, smiles from the far shore of mercy, and floats up the hall like an angel in hell.

✤ ✤ ✤

I keep thinking there is some path between resignation and resistance, a state of being that is available not simply to the person who is dying but to any man who feels death impeding and diminishing his ability to fully live. We say that death is an abstraction, that it is impossible for anyone ever to take one's own death into one's own mind, but perhaps that is in fact the task: to make death concrete, or to make concrete experience more fully alive with the hole of life-lessness that is part of one's perception of it.

One of the most powerful experiences of art that I have ever had was at a retrospective of the American artist Lee Bontecou. I went with my wife, who was not then my wife, but a woman I was falling in love with in ways I had never imagined, ways that were palpably and frighteningly changing my imagination, and when we both began spontaneously crying in the last room of the exhibit, our reaction seemed to seal that love at its deepest junctures. I'm not a sentimental person. I don't think I've *ever* cried over a work of art before. Nor is Bontecou a sentimental artist. Indeed, part of what is so moving about her work is the sense of enclosed and solitary suffering that is slowly transfigured through the decades (you feel it underneath the social suffering, feel a single existential being struggling for meaning in the midst of immense, meaningless, inchoate, and seemingly all-controlling social and historical pressures). Powerful early work of brute, mechanistic, militaristic obduracy gives way to a period of (strikingly less successful) investigative whimsy. It is as if she's wandering in the desert for a number of years, and then, still very much in the desert (the fact of emptiness, of absence, undergirds the assertions of the late work), a revelation comes: we walked into a room filled with large, delicate, astonishingly complex mobiles that hung from the ceiling—like sea creatures or dream creatures; we knew, at any rate, that we were suddenly in another element. And could breathe.

Death, for a young artist, is a common fixation because it seems to offer a source of intensity and power to which the artist otherwise would have no access. Death usually has a thematic feel to it in these instances, as in early Stevens ("Death is the mother of beauty"). It is an idea, not a sensation. There are three ways for this fixation to play out. If the artist is unlucky but strong and gets a conscious taste of death well before his time, then death may very well enter the work as sensation, may insinuate itself into the textures and materials of the art (Keats). If, on the other hand, he is lucky as a person but weak minded as an artist, then he will either dissipate his energies into frivolity or continue to hammer at death like a gong until his work is nothing but hollow reverberations (Swinburne). A third option, and the most mature vision, occurs when death and life are so woven together that they are completely indistinguishable: you cannot see one without the other.

Lee Bontecou is in this third category, finally, though early on, death, for her, is pure theme. The very bulkiness of her first sculptures betrays this fixity, this misplaced devotion; the later work shreds everything to air and light and wire and glass, as if the souls of the former pieces had been lifted out of the corrupted bodies. And yet something essential remains. In every single sculpture from Bontecou's early work there is a hole, a space of utter blackness. The holes aren't included within the sculptures so much as inflicted upon them. They are expressions—the word seems wrong, for they are pre-expressive—of meaninglessness, little abysses that contain every last bit of the nothing that is space.

The holes are in the late mobiles too. You have to look a bit to see them because the entire pieces are in a sense full of holes, and the singular expressions are very much a part of that total transparency. But they are there in every one, just as in the earliest pieces: that inexplicable, irreducible, and necessary hole that no art, this art clearly says, can ever completely fill. I remember thinking that day of William Empson:

> Imagine, then, by miracle, with me,
> (Ambiguous gifts, as what gods give must be)
> What could not possibly be there,
> And learn a style from a despair.

And I remember, too, thinking that I was seeing a model for how to live, for how to be conscious in the world at that time. It took a few years—in fact, it took until the writing of this very paragraph—for me to realize that the art was also giving me a model for how to die.

But still, this is art, not life. This is a little epiphany in a sunlit museum with someone I had fallen in love with, not the wintry, warrened world of the cancer floor of Northwestern Memorial Hospital, where, it sometimes seems, I now live. Art can model the more difficult dynamic of transfiguring one's life, but at some point the dynamic reverses itself: *life* models, or forces, the existential crisis by which art—great art—is fully experienced. There is a fluidity between art and life, then, in the same way that there is, in the best lives, a fluidity between mind and matter, self and soul, life and death. There are lives that experience seems to stream clearly through, rather than getting slowed and clogged up in the drift waste of ego or stagnating in little inlets of despair, envy, rage. It has to do with seizing and releasing as a single gesture. It has to do with standing in relation to life and death as those late Bontecou mobiles do, owning an emptiness that, because you have claimed it, has become a source of light, wearing your wound that, like a ramshackle house on some high, exposed hill, sings with the hard wind that is steadily destroying it.

❖ ❖ ❖

When my grandmother—whose reading was limited to the Bible and *Guideposts*, and whose life was circumscribed by the tiny yard around her tiny house in tiny Colorado City, Texas—died twenty years ago, I was pierced, not simply by grief and the loss of her presence, but by a sense that some very particular and hard-won kind of consciousness had gone out of the world. I mentioned this earlier: there is a kind of consciousness that is not consciousness as intellectuals define it. It is passive rather than active; it involves allowing the world to stream through you rather than you always reaching out to take hold of it. It is the consciousness of the work of art and not necessarily of the artist who made it. People, occasionally, can be such works, creation streaming through them like the inspiration that, in truth, all of creation is.

✤ ✤ ✤

I felt a million living tendrils
rooting through the thing I was,
as if I'd turned to earth before my death
or in my death could somehow feel.

✤ ✤ ✤

Lee Bontecou, my wife, my grandmother—if this consciousness I'm describing is gendered (and I think it is), it is clearly feminine. The single most damaging and distorting thing that religion has done to faith involves overlooking, undervaluing, and even outright suppressing this interior, ulterior kind of consciousness. So much Western theology has been constructed on a fundamental disfigurement of the mind and reality. In neglecting the voices of women, who are more attuned to the immanent nature of divinity, who feel that eruption in their very bodies, theology has silenced a powerful—perhaps the most powerful—side of God.

✤ ✤ ✤

If Thou be more than hate or atmosphere,
Step forth in splendor, mortify our wolves,
Or we assume a sovereignty ourselves.
       —GWENDOLYN BROOKS, "GOD WORKS
                IN A MYSTERIOUS WAY"

Too late? Think of the confident, amnesiac authority of modern science (haven't we been here before?). Think of all the cultural emphasis on the self. Think even of theologians (Karl Barth, for example)
who preach fervently against human "sovereignty," who argue for the
absolute otherness of God: all too often they do so with an assurance
that amounts to an implicit claim of just such sovereignty.

⊹ ⊹ ⊹

> The nearest friends can go
> With anyone to death, comes so far short
> They might as well not try to go at all.
> No, from the time when one is sick to death,
> One is alone, and he dies more alone.
> Friends make pretense of following to the grave,
> But before one is in it, their minds are turned
> And making the best of their way back to life
> And living people, and things they understand.

Robert Frost. From his great poem "Home Burial." The speaker is
the mother of a dead child; she is speaking to the child's father,
who has not grieved in any way that she has been able to perceive
or understand. There is something hysterical in her accusations of
him, and also (this is what makes the poem so great) something
true—and not simply true to her own situation (I think the father
has felt great grief, but he has walled it in; she is justified in banging on the walls) but more generally true as well. Everyone is in
his life to the uttermost. That clamor in your head, that endless
quick-fire free association whose engine is ego, that blood compulsion in the brain beating onward, onward, onward: this is going on in
the minds of seven billion people on the planet, in seven billion completely singular and, it can often seem, completely sealed-in ways. It is
one thing to recognize this intellectually; it is quite another to have

it brought home to you at the edge of death—your own or someone else's.

I'm a Christian not because of the resurrection (I wrestle with this), and not because I think Christianity contains more truth than other religions (I think God reveals himself, or herself, in many forms, some not religious), and not simply because it was the religion in which I was raised (this has been a high barrier). I am a Christian because of that moment on the cross when Jesus, drinking the very dregs of human bitterness, cries out, *My God, my God, why hast thou forsaken me?* (I know, I know: he was quoting the Psalms, and who quotes a poem when being tortured? The words aren't the point. The point is that he felt human destitution to its absolute degree; the point is that God is *with us*, not beyond us, in suffering.) I am a Christian because I understand that moment of Christ's passion to have meaning in my own life, and what it means is that the absolutely solitary and singular nature of extreme human pain is an illusion. I'm not suggesting that ministering angels are going to come down and comfort you as you die. I'm suggesting that Christ's suffering shatters the iron walls around individual human suffering, that Christ's compassion makes extreme human compassion—to the point of death, even—possible. Human love *can* reach right into death, then, but not if it is *merely* human love.

Such a realization should ease loneliness—even for the griever who is left alone; it should also, in time, help to propel one back into life. Nothing is served by following someone into a grave. Somehow, even deep within extreme grief, the worst pain is knowing that your pain will pass, all the sharp particulars of life that one person's presence made possible will fade into mere memory, and then not even that. Consequently, many people fight hard to keep their wound fresh, for in the wound, at least, is the loss, and in the loss the life you shared. Or so it seems. In truth the life you shared, because it *was* shared, was marked by joy, by light. Cradled in loneliness, it becomes pure grief, pure shadow, which is a problem not simply for the present and the future, but for the past as well. Excessive grief, the kind that paralyzes a person, the kind that eventually becomes an entire personality—in the end this does not honor the love that is its origin. *Is*, not was: our dead have presence. You don't need to believe in some literal heaven to feel the ways in which the dead inhabit us—for good, if we will let them do that, which means, paradoxically, letting them go.

"But the world's evil," cries out the woman in "Home Burial." "I won't have grief so / If I can change it. Oh, I won't, I won't." She's right: the world is evil, and grief is too little acknowledged and honored in our culture. But I have a feeling that I'm speaking here to people who, like this woman, are conscious of this fact and determined to resist it. I don't know if the woman in "Home Burial" is pathological; I don't think so. What I do know, or sense, is that within the love that once opened up the world to you—from the birth of a child to meeting your mate—is a key that can let you back into the world when that love is gone.

✤ ✤ ✤

Despite all that I have gone through, and despite all that I now face, I am still struck by the singular nature of the pain in the weeks after my diagnosis. It was not simply the fact itself searing through all the circumstances of my life, nor was it, as many people might suspect, the full impact of meaninglessness, the arbitrary nature of our existence, the utter illusion of God. No, it was an excess of meaning for which I had no context. It was the world burning to be itself beyond my ruined eyes. It was God straining through matter to make me see, and to grant me the grace of simple praise.

✤ ✤ ✤

Whenever I find myself answering someone's questions about my illness, explaining what is going on in my body or the bizarre treatments I am about to undergo, it is as if I am wholly detached from what I am describing, as if my body were some third thing to which both of us were impassively directing our attention. This is one reason why any expression of pity can be so jarring and unwelcome. The sick person becomes very adept at distinguishing between compassion and pity. Compassion is someone else's suffering flaring in your own nerves. Pity is a projection of, a lament for, the self. All those people weeping in the mirror of your misery? Their tears are real, but they are not for you.

✣ ✣ ✣

At the moment which is not of action or inaction
You can receive this: "on whatever sphere of being
The mind of a man may be intent
At the time of death"—that is the one action
(And the time of death is every moment)
Which shall fructify in the lives of others:
And do not think of the fruit of action.
Fare forward.

—T. S. ELIOT, "THE DRY SALVAGES"

Always that little caveat, that little appeal to relevance: *And the time of death is every moment*. Let me tell you, it is qualitatively different when death leans over to sniff you, when massive unmetaphorical pain goes crawling through your bones, when fear—goddamn fear, you can't get rid of it—ices your spine. Saint Teresa, describing one's entry into one of the innermost rooms of the "interior castle," into the domain of mystical experience, says, "It's necessary that he who gives everything else give the courage also." She means God. And God has given me courage in the past—I have felt palpably lifted beyond my own ability to respond or react. But this most recent time in the hospital, when the cancer had become so much more aggressive and it seemed for a time as if I'd reached the end of my options, I felt only death. In retrospect it seems like a large and ominous failure.

✤ ✤ ✤

Or maybe I have simply been given another chance ("I lose / courage but courage is not lost" —Geoffrey Hill). Here is a poem by Eugenio Montale that I found myself returning to in the hospital:

> The red lily, if one day
> it took root in your twenty-year-old heart
> (the weir was sparkling
> under the sand-diggers' sieves,
> sleek moles dove and burrowed in the rushes,
> towers, flags withstood the rain,
> and the happy graft in the new sun
> knit without your knowing);
>
> the red lily, long since sacrificed
> on far-off crags to mistletoe
> that scintillates your scarf and hands
> with an incorruptible chill—
> ditchflower that will unfurl for you
> on those solemn banks where the hum of time
> no longer wearies us . . . : to strike
> the harp of heaven, make death a friend.
>
> —"THE RED LILY," TRANSLATION
> BY JONATHAN GALASSI

Knit without your knowing. Or knit, we might say, without the kind of knowing that we usually call knowing; knit in the kind of conscious unconsciousness that infuses Lee Bontecou's work, that made my grandmother an avatar of existential philosophy, though she never offered any of it out loud. She didn't need to, any more than Montale's wild lily does. This is a poem about the way in which a single experience, a single sensation, can, if we are faithful to it, return to us through the years, can serve as ballast against the hard weathers that will surely come. It is a poem about loving the earth so intensely that leaving it provokes no fear, partly because to love the earth with such devotion is to assent to its terms, and partly because such love awakens the soul that—in some way, with form or without—survives. *The soul.* It is a poem about that too, for Montale had a religious sensibility, though little patience for religious structures. The poem posits a place "where the hum of time / no longer wearies us," and slowly we realize that those banks are the banks of Lethe, and the only chill that is "incorruptible" is the chill of death, which the poem welcomes, in its way, with open arms. I take comfort from it, even if it was written by a poet for whom death was still mostly a theme.

❖ ❖ ❖

The girls come clambering into bed at 6:00 a.m. laughing, electrically recognizing with little shocks all the solid objects that have survived the night: pillow, nose, ear, boom-boom (car), arf-arf (a very patient poodle). The girls go running at dusk back into the master bedroom trying to avoid going to bed, and when I swoop them up from behind, they laugh with all the pure hilarity of the souls that are still transparent in them, shining out of their skin like light you see nowhere except sometimes in the sacred radiance of someone who is dying well. It is as if joy were the default setting of human emotion, not the furtive, fugitive glimpses it becomes in lives compromised by necessity, familiarity, "maturity," suffering. You must become as little children, Jesus said, a statement that is often used to justify anti-intellectualism and the renunciation of reason, but which I take actually to mean that we must recover this sense of wonder, this excess of spirit brimming out of the body. William Wordsworth knew this, and in fact intuited an afterlife from the intensity of children's sensibilities, who live not as if divinity were immanent in everything around them, but in full possession of, in full *consciousness* of—consciousness in the sense I have been describing, what we are prone to call unconsciousness—miraculous matter:

> O joy! that in our embers
> Is something that doth live,
> That Nature yet remembers
> What was so fugitive!
> The thought of our past years in me doth breed
> Perpetual benediction: not indeed
> For that which is most worthy to be blest,
> Delight and liberty, the simple creed
> Of Childhood, whether busy or at rest,
> With new-fledged hope still fluttering in his breast—
> Not for these I raise
> The song of thanks and praise;
> But for those obstinate questionings
> Of sense and outward things,
> Fallings from us, vanishings,
> Blank misgivings of a Creature
> Moving about in worlds not realized,
> High instincts, before which our mortal Nature
> Did tremble like a guilty Thing surprised:
> But for those first affections,
> Those shadowy recollections,
> Which, be they what they may,
> Are yet the fountain-light of all our day,
> Are yet a master-light of all our seeing;

Uphold us, cherish, and have power to make
Our noisy years seem moments in the being
Of the eternal Silence.
　　—FROM "ODE: INTIMATIONS OF IMMORTALITY"

✥ ✥ ✥

My loves, I will be with you, even if I am not with you. Every day I feel a little more the impress of eternity, learn a little more "the discipline of suffering which leads to peace of the spirit," as T. S. Eliot said, writing of the seventeenth-century poet and priest George Herbert (read him!), who died when he was thirty-nine and had only recently found true happiness with his new wife and new commitment to God. My loves, I love you with all the volatility and expansiveness of spirit that you have taught me to feel, and I feel your futures opening out from you, and in those futures I know my own. I will be with you. I will comfort you in your despair and I will share in your joy. They need not be only grief, only pain, these black holes in our lives. If we can learn to live not merely with them but by means of them, if we can let them be part of the works of sacred art that we in fact are, then these apparent weaknesses can be the very things that strengthen us. Life tears us apart, but through those wounds, if we have tended them, love may enter us. It may be the love of someone you have lost. It may be the love of your own spirit for the self that at times you think you hate. However it comes though, in all these—of all these and yet more than they, so much more—there burns the abiding love of God. But if you find that you cannot believe in God, then do not worry yourself with it. No one can say what names or forms God might take, nor gauge the intensity of unbelief we may need to wake up our souls. My love is still true, my children, still with you, still straining through your ambitions and your disappointments, your frenzies and forgetfulness, through all the glints and gulfs of implacable matter—to reach you, to help you, to heal you.

✦ ✦ ✦

How strange, that all
The terrors, pains, and early miseries,
Regrets, vexations, lassitudes interfused
Within my mind, should e'er have borne a part,
And that a needful part, in making up
The calm existence that is mine when I
Am worthy of myself!

—WILLIAM WORDSWORTH,
FROM "THE PRELUDE"

✦ ✦ ✦

The temptation is to make an idol of our own experience, to assume our pain is more singular than it is. Even here, in some of the entries above, I see that I have fallen prey to it. In truth, experience means nothing if it does not mean beyond itself: *we* mean nothing unless and until our hard-won meanings are internalized and catalyzed within the lives of others. There is something I am meant to see, something for which my own situation and suffering are the lens, but the cost of such seeing—I am just beginning to realize—may very well be any final clarity or perspective on my own life, my own faith. That would not be a bad fate, to burn up like the booster engine that falls away from the throttling rocket, lighting a little dark as I go.

A MILLION LITTLE OBLIVIONS

"Spots of time," Wordsworth called them, those moments when something in the world, something *of* the world—even as that something reveals some intuitive, and sometimes even intolerable, beyond—is made manifest; and not only made manifest but given agency, animation, *attention*.

Last night my wife and I finally fell asleep after talking and crying about our life together and the life of our children—the splendor of some moments, so many moments, the gift we have been given; and then the misery of my sickness and the way it is crushing us, the terror the two of us feel at what will happen if (I won't write "when," but we are now always thinking it) I die.

I wake in the night with a terror that is purer, further than my own. My suffering is the key but not the content, and for an hour I am silvered with an icy, infinite distance, an abyss of pure meaninglessness of which I am merely some small and dreadfully sentient particle. I am not dreaming. I have never been more awfully awake. A spot of time, and what the spot shows, this time, is nothingness, suffering without meaning.

✦ ✦ ✦

It is not some meditative communion with God that I crave. What one wants during extreme crisis is not connection with God, but connection with people; not supernatural love, but human love. No, that is not quite right. What one craves is supernatural love, but one finds it only within human love. This is why I am, such as I am, a Christian, because I can feel God only through physical existence, can feel his love only in the love of other people. I believe in grace and chance, at the same time. I believe in absolute truth and absolute contingency, at the same time. And I believe that Christ is the seam soldering together these wholes that our half vision—and our entire clock-bound, logic-locked way of life—shapes as polarities.

❖ ❖ ❖

Sometimes it seems that I can happily hold all Christian tenets in an active abeyance, a fusion of faith and skepticism that includes and transcends literal and figurative truths, if I can hold fast to one indestructible fact (*fact?!*): Christ's resurrection. This event answers every impulse, fear, and need of my imagination, quiets and clarifies the raucous onslaught of time, suffers me—the mute, destitute, unselfed seed of being that is most me—to understand what suffering is, and what it means. But no. The reality wavers, the image fades like a reflection on the water, for under every assertion about God, including the one I am making at this very minute, the ground gives way, and once again I am left with the vital and futile truth that to live in faith is to live like the Jesus lizard, quick and nimble on the water into which a moment's pause would make it sink.

❖ ❖ ❖

Christ. He won't go away. An editor objected to one of these chapters because there was "too much Christ" in it, but I always feel that I am evading Christ, avoiding him, almost as if I am, with the old liberal Protestant reticence that masks a fundamental impotence, embarrassed by him. And yet there is an intensity there to which I can hardly bear to turn, a torn place in my soul, a blood rupture. He is not my "friend."

In church much is made of Christ as a moral exemplar, but I find this not only problematic (How could he treat his mother so harshly? Why such impatience with, and even baiting of, his disciples? And what about that comment about the ubiquitous poor?) but also just generally useless. It's the Jeffersonian Christ, but you hardly need Christ to model the virtues that Jefferson had in mind. No, to be a Christian has to mean believing in the resurrected Christ, though I grow less and less interested in the historical argument around this: Did a man named Jesus really rise from the dead three days after being crucified in Jerusalem two thousand years ago? The arguments are compelling on both sides, but the whole process of putting faith on trial, the incessant need for an intellectual *result*, feels false to me. It seems like a failure of vision even to ask the question, much less to get all tangled up in it.

⁜ ⁜ ⁜

There is a moment in Acts when the apostle Paul is reproving the Athenians who have set up an altar—very much in line with our own times, this—"TO THE UNKNOWN GOD." Paul says that God is in fact always near us if we will simply learn to look, and then he says something, just a few decades after the death of Christ, that is notable and powerful for its utter lack of historicity: "in Christ we live, and move, and have our being." Paul is trying to get those Athenians—or, more likely, his own early followers—to see the life of Christ as not merely a point in time but as a portal to eternity. He is trying to get them to see what I must see: that Christ's life is not simply a model for how to live, but the living truth of my own existence. Christ is not alive now because he rose from the dead two thousand years ago. He rose from the dead two thousand years ago because he is alive right now.

⁜ ⁜ ⁜

Fear. Of nothingness. Of dying. Of failure. Of change. It is of different degrees, but it all comes from one source, which is the isolated self, the self willfully held apart from God. There are three ways you can deal with this fear. You can simply refuse to acknowledge it, dulling your concerns with alcohol or entertainment or exercise or even a sort of virtuous busyness, adding your own energies to the white noise of anxiety that this culture we have created seems to use as fuel. This is despair, but it is a quiet despair, and bearable for many years. By the time that great grinding wheel of the world rolls over you for good, you will be too eroded to notice.

Or, if you are strong in the way the world is strong, you can strap yourself into life and give yourself over to a kind of furious resistance that may very well carry you through your travails, may bring you great success and seem to the world triumphant, perhaps even heroic. But if it is merely your will that you are asserting, then you will develop a carapace around your soul, the soul that God is trying to refine, and one day you will turn to dust inside that shell that you have made.

There is another way. It is the way of Christ in the Garden of Gethsemane, pleading for release from his fate, abandoned by God. It is something you cannot learn as a kind of lesson simply from reading the text. Christ teaches by example, true, but he lives with us, lives in us, through imagination and experience. It is through all these trials in our own lives, these fears however small, that we come close to Christ, if we can learn to say, with him, "not my will, Lord, but yours." This is in no way resignation, for Christ still had to act. We all have to act, whether it's against the fears of our daily life or against the fear that life itself is in danger of being destroyed. And when we act in the will of God, we express hope in its purest and most powerful form, for hope, as Václav Havel has said, is a condition of your soul, not a response to the circumstances in which you find yourself. Hope is what Christ had in the garden, though he had no reason for it in terms of events, and hope is what he has right now, in the garden of our own griefs.

❖ ❖ ❖

(The mother of a preacher I know presented him with her will. It contained detailed instructions for her funeral, which culminated with this: "Not much Christ." My friend replied: "Not much afterlife." I like to think of Christ—and I *can* think of him—laughing.)

❖ ❖ ❖

The problem with so much thinking about Christ's resurrection and the promise that lies therein is the self-concern that is attendant upon, and often driving, this thought: resurrection matters because we matter, our individual selves; it matters because it is *for us*. But Christ's death and resurrection ought to be a means of freeing us from precisely this kind of thinking, this notion of, and regard for, the self, which is the source of so much of our suffering and unhappiness. ("To hoard the self is to grow a colossal sense for the futility of living."—Abraham Joshua Heschel) Instead, contemporary Christianity all too often preaches an idea of resurrection that is little more than a means of projecting our paltry selves ad infinitum, and the result is a grinning, self-aggrandizing, ironclad kind of happiness that has no truth in it.

❖ ❖ ❖

You must let go of all conception of what eternity *is*, which means letting go of who *you* are, in order to feel the truth of eternity and its meaning in your life—and in your death.

✤ ✤ ✤

Falling in love seems at the same time an intensification of consciousness and the loss of it. Never are the physical facts of existence more apparent and cherished, and never is their impermanence more obvious and painful. One is reduced and exalted to one's senses at the same time, an animal spirit, a spiritual animal. This experience brings most of us closer to a knowledge of God than anything else in our lives, which is to say, closer to that unknowingness that heightens and haunts every aspect of our lives, and is our death. For that's what we feel when we feel most alive, the bite (it may not be conscious at all) of life's ending. To love is to enter this terror, to revel in it, and even, for a time, to triumph over it. And might there be some ultimate analogue to this experience, wherein what we imagine is pure oblivion is actually some immense, unimaginable, and utterly specific attention turning toward us, as the force that scours us out of this existence loves us into another. I'm not sure there's much comfort to be had from this thought, at least not the sort of comfort that religion promises. The only thing more absurd than categorically denying all life beyond this one is attempting to describe or have some sense of that life, for this is not consciousness, but its end, in both senses of that word, not love as we have ever known it, but love as being finally, fully known.

✤ ✤ ✤

FOR D.

Groans going all the way up a young tree
half-cracked and caught in the crook of another

pause. All around the hill-ringed, heavened pond
leaves shush themselves like an audience.

A cellular stillness, as of some huge attention
bearing down. May I hold your hand?

A clutch of mayflies banqueting on oblivion
writhes above the water like visible light.

❖ ❖ ❖

The task is not to "believe" in a life beyond this one; the task is to
perceive it. Perception is not projection: we are not meant to project
our experience of this life into another, nor are we meant to imagine, by means of the details of this life (which is the only resource we
have for imagining), some impossible beyond. Life is not life without
an afterlife, and there is no afterlife beyond the life we treasure and
suffer and feel slipping from us moment by moment. I don't mean
to hide within an impenetrable paradox. I mean to say something
along the lines of what Paul Éluard said a century ago: "There is
another world, but it is in this one." Or, more to the point, Christ
two thousand years ago: "The kingdom of God is within you." We
cannot get beyond our lives until we eliminate all notions and expectations of a "beyond." No one ever believed in God before perceiving God:

An aching prodigal
Who would make miracles
To understand the simple given.
——JAY WRIGHT, "BEGINNING
AGAIN"

❖ ❖ ❖

But oh, how fugitive those miracles, how implacable and relentless
the given. What might "success" mean to such a lifelong and in

some way eternally suspended search? Could such a mind and heart even handle the onrush of rapture?

4.

For, what with my whole world-wide wandering,
  What with my search drawn out thro' years, my hope
  Dwindled into a ghost not fit to cope
With that obstreperous joy success would bring,—
I hardly tried now to rebuke the spring
  My heart made, finding failure in its scope.

These lines are from "Childe Roland to the Dark Tower Came" by Robert Browning and were written more than a hundred and fifty years ago. They are about a knight, who for Browning is obviously a spiritual knight, a knight of the soul, or a knight in search of a soul at the center of existence:

5.

As when a sick man very near to death
  Seems dead indeed, and feels begin and end
  The tears and takes the farewell of each friend,
And hears one bid the other go, draw breath
Freelier outside, ("since all is o'er," he saith,
  "And the blow fall'n no grieving can amend;")

6.

While some discuss if near the other graves
  Be room enough for this, and when a day
  Suits best for carrying the corpse away,
With care about the banners, scarves and staves,—

And still the man hears all, and only craves
He may not shame such tender love and stay.

7.

Thus, I had so long suffered in this quest,
  Heard failure prophesied so oft, been writ
  So many times among "The Band"—to wit,
The knights who to the Dark Tower's search addressed
Their steps—that just to fail as they, seemed best,
  And all the doubt was now—should I be fit.

To be fit for failure. It's a modest ambition, a defeated ambition, really. Or at least it seems so. The knight staggers on through a land in which "penury, inertness, and grimace, / In some strange sort, were the land's portion." He turns his thoughts inward for strength and is briefly fortified by memories of other knights on other quests, their bravery and honor, which only manage to sting him worse as he remembers then the ignoble ends to which those knights eventually came. "Better this present than a past like that."

And isn't that always the case? Better this present than the past in which we remember falling away from those moments when we felt God in us, or those moments when we believed so strongly in the belief of someone else that we were lifted up ourselves—any shining, shattering instant when life claimed us, calmed us, and despair and death were at bay.

Gone. It is always—it will always be—gone.

And poetry itself? It would seem that art at least would provide refuge and possibility for Browning. In the same year that he wrote "Childe Roland" he responded to a criticism from John Ruskin (about another poem) with a fierce but winningly playful defense of the enduring mysteries of the art to which he'd given his life:

You ought, I think, to keep pace with the thought tripping from ledge to ledge of my "glaciers," as you call them; not stand poking your alpenstock into the holes, and demonstrating that no foot could have stood there;—suppose it *sprang* over there?

There was no quit in him. But he was forty-three years old when he wrote "Childe Roland." He was known primarily as Elizabeth Barrett Browning's husband, and for all the otherworldly insight and umbrage he expressed to Ruskin—"A poet's affair is with God, to whom he is accountable, and of whom is his reward; look elsewhere, and you find misery enough"—it's obvious that like any human, he *did* look elsewhere for confirmation and did find "misery enough." The public failure of his art turned him inward, and made that old effort of "putting the infinite within the finite" seem more hectic and hell-bent than peaceful or releasing. For evidence, you need only read the words of this direly determined knight (note especially the pun on "mews"; these may be knights he's describing, but they are also poets):

22

Glad was I when I reached the other bank.
  Now for a better country. Vain presage!
  Who were the strugglers, what war did they wage
Whose savage trample thus could pad the dank
Soil to a plash? Toads in a poisoned tank,
  Or wild cats in a red-hot iron cage—

23

The fight must so have seemed in that fell cirque.
  What kept them there, with all the plain to choose?
  No foot-print leading to that horrid mews,
None out of it; mad brewage set to work

Their brains, no doubt, like galley-slaves the Turk
Pits for his pastime, Christians against Jews.

Torture implements, blighted landscape, a great black bird like a buzzard of hell—it's the dark night of the soul, undergone by the dark knight of the soul, and just at its pith, just when the last hope and humanity have been extinguished in him, he looks up:

30

Burningly it came on me all at once,
  This was the place! Those two hills on the right
  Crouched like two bulls locked horn in horn in fight
While to the left, a tall scalped mountain. Dunce,
Fool, to be dozing at the very nonce,
  After a life spent training for the sight!

After a lifetime spent in search of the Dark Tower, it appears not only right in front of him, but so woven into the ordinary that he could easily have walked right by it. "If you are searching for God," Pascal says, "then you have found him." But were you *really* searching for that—the truth of it, I mean—and what will you do now that you've "found" it? Out of the dark tower come all the other knights who have made their way to this place—the price of entry to which, the knight realizes all too clearly, is death—and the knight's last action on this earth is the last line of the poem:

34

There they stood, ranged along the hill-sides—met
  To view the last of me, a living frame
  For one more picture! In a sheet of flame
I saw them and I knew them all. And yet

Dauntless the slug-horn to my lips I set
And blew. "Childe Roland to the Dark Tower came."

Triumph or defeat? Redemption or oblivion? The knight knows he's going to die, but he is "dauntless." He is at the edge where all human action fails, and he is acting. Auden once described poetry as "the clear expression of mixed feelings": this is the clear expression of an ambivalent action. Or no, not ambivalent. The very opposite of that, in fact. The knight's last action is inscrutable, unknowable, but it is also mysteriously decisive. It is, like a poem, so sealed in by and replete with meaning that there is nothing outside of the act to translate it: it is only—*it is utterly*—itself. To fling yourself into failure; to soar into the sadness by which you've lived; to die with neither defiance nor submission, but in some higher fusion of the two; to walk lost at the last into the arms of emptiness, crying the miracles of God.

❖ ❖ ❖

The endless, useless urge to look on life comprehensively, to take a bird's-eye view of ourselves and judge the dimensions of what we have or have not done: this is life as landscape, or life as résumé. But life is incremental, and though a worthwhile life is a gathering together of all that one is, good and bad, successful and not, the paradox is that we can never really see this one thing that all of our increments (and decrements, I suppose) add up to. "Early we receive a call," writes Czeslaw Milosz, "yet it remains incomprehensible, / and only late do we discover how obedient we were."

❖ ❖ ❖

We are each of us—every single one of us—meant to be a lens for truths that we ourselves cannot see. "The system cannot include the systematizer," Kierkegaard once said, a clunky but accurate formulation of a problem that applies even to people who don't have a philosophical bone in their bodies. Our lives burn up, and our minds within them, and all that we have sought so hard to retain in art or durable projects or familial memory. But to live in faith is to live toward a truth that we can but dimly sense, if at all, and to die in faith is to leave an afterimage whose dimensions and meanings we could never even have guessed at. Something of us—something most us, and least us—is saved and made available for others. This is as true of the politician as it is of the poet, as true of the teacher or the preacher, the mother or the father, as it is of a Danish philosopher.

❖ ❖ ❖

In the end the very things that have led us to God are the things that we must sacrifice. The capacities that we have developed and refined, that have enabled us to perceive some endlessly creative absence at the center of this life, some vitality in the void—in the end these gifts must be given entirely away, that we may be light enough for this last passage:

> No more thy meaning seek, thine anguish plead,
> But leaving straining thought and stammering word,
> Across the barren azure pass to God;
> Shooting the void in silence, like a bird,
> A bird that shuts his wings for better speed.
> —FREDERICK GODDARD TUCKERMAN, FROM
> "SONNET XXVIII"

❖ ❖ ❖

I can't keep the elegy out of this. I can't close any tighter the circle of absence and unmeaning these sentences circumscribe and seem—

even in the midst of meaning, even in the midst of joy—to mourn. I can't be the man who stands on his belief as on some stark outcrop of rock from which the land is larger, the horizon farther, every path and peril clearly seen. Word after word ekes out of me as if I were in some bare, wasted place scraping myself forward, as if there were a "forward," as if I did not end up every time on this same circle circumscribing all I do not know. I can't keep the elegy out of this, though elegy is not what I intend, not what I feel when I feel my life in all its bright particulars implying—imploring—God.

✢ ✢ ✢

Then I went out into the million little oblivions of which the day was made. Clouds collided and combined above me like brains and brief beings and then like nothing at all, and two foul-smelling peccaries snuffed and shuffled over the bristling volcanic land of which they seemed extreme instances, and in a weird little weed-cleared space the bones of five antelope lay tangled and whitened like the last leap of a single creature. I met up with my friend and we talked of the work we'd done that day, and the lives out of which that work had come, and further back the vanished lives out of which our own lives had come. We turned toward home because the dark was gathering, the cold was sharpening, but we were so deep into conversation that I hardly knew the walk was ending, as climbing step by step as from a storm cellar up from a family's madness, sadness, cold enclosure that her own mind had wrought, she said, "And yet I seem to have been given a happy soul."

✢ ✢ ✢

I have had a bone marrow transplant. I have been home from the hospital for five days. Among other "side effects," it skinned me on the inside, leaving me so bloody and abraded from mouth to bowels that I couldn't even eat an aspirin. Even worse than that, though, was the way the Armageddon dose of chemo destroyed my mind so that I was unable to read even an ordinary magazine article, unable to follow a simple drama on television. I was in the hospital for several weeks, and the hours acquired a palpable thickness to them, like a pill impossible to swallow, some "cure"—by now the word is both radiant with, and devoid of, meaning, like "faith," like "God"—you fight down at every instant because there is no other choice, you are out of options. And I am: out of options.

Seven years of cancer have certainly exposed me to wider and more searing notions of suffering (and not only my own), but I'm not sure I'm any more enlightened about what suffering means—or even, in the midst of it, when pain has obliterated my brain, *that* it means. Is this a moral failure or mystical fulfillment? Is it an achievement to reach a point at which I trust that the meaning, which I do not feel, is there, a condition that elsewhere in this book I have called faith? Or should I reach the end of an effort like this, having felt acutely the end of a life like mine (both intensely devoted and terminally confused, haunted and inhabited by a God of grief, of love, of absence, of always), with more certainty, more assurance that I am loved by God, some freedom from these cracks that open in my brain, rifts splitting right down to the bright abyss that is, finally, devoid of any meaning but the one I give it?

Ah—not to learn even what I have learned. To have to keep hammering it home. Or, more accurately, having it hammered home. (Once again: in a grain of grammar, a world of hope.) I am not "out of options." In fact, my bone marrow is, according to my last biopsy, free of cancer, and the dozens of tumors that at times have been so aggressive that I could see and feel them protruding from my skin—they have all shrunk to what my doctor says is probably just residual scar tissue. No one promises permanence. The chances are high that there is some errant malevolent cell swimming around, plotting a comeback. But there is every reason to think that I am at the beginning of a long remission, maybe five years, maybe ten, maybe even more. Even without this gift, though, this sense of promise and hope, I have allowed myself to forget all the wonders and clarities that have come to me this past year, which has been a solid year of suffering and the sharp sense of death. I waste too much time in the little lightless caverns of my own mind. So much of faith has so little to do with belief, and so much to do with acceptance. Acceptance of all the gifts that God, even in the midst of death, grants us. Acceptance of the fact that we are, as Paul Tillich says, accepted. Acceptance of grace.

Grace. It is—not at all coincidentally, I now think—the name of the street where my wife and I first lived together. It is the middle name of our firstborn child, who with her twin sister has taught us so much about how to accept God's immanent presence. And it is, I am absolutely sure, the fearful and hopeful state in which my wife and I lay the first night I was home from the hospital after the transplant, feeling like a holy fever that bright defiance of, not death exactly, and not suffering, but meaningless death and suffering—which surely warrants, if anything does, the name of faith.

My God my bright abyss
into which all my longing will not go
once more I come to the edge of all I know
and believing nothing believe in this.

ACKNOWLEDGMENTS

I am grateful to the editors of the following magazines, in which sections from this book originally appeared:

The American Scholar
The Best American Spiritual Writing (2008, 2010)
The Chicagoan
The Christian Century
Commonweal
Harvard Divinity Bulletin
The Huffington Post
Image
Poem (England)
Poetry Review (England)
Pushcart Prize (2009)

I'm especially grateful to Naeem Murr and Paul Elie for their help with this book.

All unattributed poems, as well as the translations of Osip Mandelstam, are my own.

The translation of the passage from Anna Kamieńska's *Diaries* was done by Clare Cavanagh and first appeared in *Poetry*.

Two entries from "God's Truth Is Life" and one from "Varieties of Quiet" are reprinted from my book *Ambition and Survival: Becoming a Poet* with the permission of The Permissions Company, Inc., on behalf of Copper Canyon Press.

Grateful acknowledgment is also made for permission to reprint excerpts from the following previously published material:

W. B. Yeats, "The Wheel." Reprinted with the permission of Scribner, a Division of Simon & Schuster, Inc., from *The Collected Works of W. B. Yeats, volume I: The Poems, Revised* by W. B. Yeats, edited by Richard J. Finneran. Copyright © 1928 by The Macmillan Company, renewed 1956 by George Yeats. All rights reserved.

Richard Wilbur, "Teresa." Excerpt from "Teresa" from *Collected Poems 1943–2004* by Richard Wilbur. Copyright © 2004 by Richard Wilbur. Reprinted by permission of Houghton Mifflin Harcourt Publishing Company. All rights reserved.

Richard Wilbur, "Hamlen Brook." "Hamlen Brook" from *Collected Poems 1943–2004* by Richard Wilbur. Copyright © 2004 by Richard Wilbur. Reprinted by permission of Houghton Mifflin Harcourt Publishing Company. All rights reserved.

Gwendolyn Brooks, "God Works in a Mysterious Way." Reprinted by consent of Brooks Permissions.

D. H. Lawrence, "There Are No Gods." Reproduced by permission of Pollinger Limited and The Estate of Frieda Lawrence Ravagli.

Craig Arnold, "Meditation on a Grapefruit." Reprinted by permission of the Estate of Craig Arnold.

Robert Bringhurst, "These Poems, She Said." From *The Beauty of the Weapons: Selected Poems 1972–1982*. Copyright © 1982 by Robert Bringhurst. Reprinted with the permission of The Permissions Company, Inc., on behalf of Copper Canyon Press (U.S.). Reprinted by permission of Gaspereau Press (Canada and unlicensed territories). Reprinted by permission of Random House UK (United Kingdom and Commonwealth, excluding Canada and unlicensed territories).

Christian Wiman, "Poŝtolka." From *Hard Night.* Copyright © 2005 by Christian Wiman. Reprinted with the permission of The Permissions Company, Inc., on behalf of Copper Canyon Press.

William Empson, "The Last Pain." From *The Complete Poems* by William Empson. Reprinted by permission of Penguin UK.

Geoffrey Hill, excerpts from "Two Chorale-Preludes" and "Lachrimae." Fom *New & Collected Poems. 1952–1992* by Geoffrey Hill. Copyright © 1994 by Geoffrey Hill. Reprinted by permission of Houghton Mifflin Harcourt Publishing Company and Penguin UK. All rights reserved.

Anna Kamienska, excerpt from *Notebooks*, translated by Clare Cavanagh. Reprinted by permission of Clare Cavanagh.

Paul Celan, "Psalm," translated by Cid Corman. From *Paul Celan: Selections*, by Paul Celan, edited by Pierre Joris, © 2005 by the Regents of the University of California. Published by the University of California Press.

René Char, "The Gods Are Back," translated by Peter Boyle. Reprinted by permission of Peter Boyle.

Robert Frost, excerpt from "The Wind and the Rain." Reprinted by arrangement with Henry Holt and Company, LLC.

Patrick Kavanagh, excerpts from "Innocence," "Having Confessed," "Canal Bank Walk," and "Auditors In." Reprinted by permission of Jonathan Williams Literary Agency.

Osip Mandelstam, excerpts from "Night Piece," "You Have Stolen My Ocean," "And I Was Alive," and "Tristia," translated by Christian Wiman. From *Stolen Air: Selected Poems of Osip Mandelstam* © 2012 by Christian Wiman. Reprinted by permission of Ecco, an imprint of HarperCollins Publishers.

Zbigniew Herbert, excerpt from "The Stars' Chosen One," translated by John and Bogdana Carpenter. From *Elegy for the Departure* © 1999. Reprinted by permission of Ecco, an imprint of Harper-Collins Publishers.

Rainer Maria Rilke, excerpt from "The Seventh Elegy," translated by Stephen Mitchell. From *The Selected Poetry of Rainer Maria Rilke* by Rainer Maria Rilke, translated by Stephen Mitchell, translation copyright © 1980, 1981, 1982 by Stephen Mitchell. Used by permission of Random House, Inc. Any third party use of this material, outside of this publication, is prohibited. Interested parties must apply directly to Random House, Inc., for permission.

Reprinted by permission of Farrar, Straus and Giroux, LLC: "Clearances II" from *Opened Ground: Selected Poems 1966–1996* by Seamus Heaney, copyright © 1998 by Seamus Heaney. "Thrushes" from *Collected Poems* by Ted Hughes, copyright © 2003 by The Estate of Ted Hughes. "Aubade" from *The Complete Poems of Philip Larkin* by Philip Larkin, edited by Archie Burnett, copyright © 2012 by The Estate of Philip Larkin. "The red lily, if one day" by Eugenio Montale, translated by Jonathan Galassi, from *Collected Poems 1920–1954* by Eugenio Montale, translated and edited by Jonathan Galassi; translation copyright © 1998, 2000, 2012 by Jonathan Galassi. "Commute (1.)," "Commute (2.)," "For D.," "From a Window," and "It is good to sit even in a rotting body," from *Every Riven Thing* by Christian Wiman, copyright © 2011 by Christian Wiman.